F

I'M ON MY WAY BUT YOUR FOOT IS ON MY HEAD

*A Black Woman's Story
of Getting Over Life's Hurdles*

Bertice Berry, Ph.D.

Previously published as
Bertice: The World According to Me

A FIRESIDE BOOK
PUBLISHED BY SIMON & SCHUSTER

FIRESIDE
Rockefeller Center
1230 Avenue of the Americas
New York, NY 10020

First Fireside Edition 1997

Previously published as *Bertice: The World According to Me*.

FIRESIDE and colophon are trademarks of Simon & Schuster Inc.

Manufactured in the United States of America

1   3   5   7   9   10   8   6   4   2

Library of Congress Cataloging-in-Publication Data
Berry, Bertice.
I'm on my way but your foot is on my head : a black woman's story of getting over life's hurdles /
Bertice Berry
p. cm.
Originally published: Bertice. New York : Scribner, 1996.
"A Fireside Book."
1. Berry, Bertice. 2. Television personalities—United States—Biography.
3. Comedians—United States—Biography. I. Title.
PN1992.4.B46A3 1997
791.45'028'092—dc21
[B]   96-54610
CIP

ISBN 0-684-81457-9
ISBN 0-684-83140-6 (pbk)

*This book is dedicated
to my ancestors,
whose spirits still fight
for my freedom.*

Acknowledgments

My sister Chris is always telling me that I give other people too much credit for what I've accomplished on my own. She's just being a proud sister. In truth, everyone I've ever met and every experience I've had, positive or negative, has been responsible for who I am and what I've written here. Some of them are included in this story, but there are too many people to talk about them all.

On the literary tip, there are those I'd like to acknowledge: Susan Moldow for being one of the few people left in the publishing business to look beyond her desk for more work.

Now, imagine working with someone who's been through what you've been through at the same time you went through it. Imagine the support you'd get. Imagine that that person truly knows her job and does it well. Think of all that you'd accomplish. Thanks Leigh Haber for being just that kind of soul sister and for seeing this through. To Greer Kessel and Jeff Wilson for being the kind of folks every publishing house should have. Thanks for being real.

To my sister/agent, Victoria (Hebuckle) Sanders, for knowing that I had a story to tell and that I needed to be the one to tell it, and for fighting with my movers and sending me bagels all on the same day: Thank you, sister.

Acknowledgments

To Dr. Bernita Berry, Sol Feldman, and Matt Sartwell, whose God-sent editorial work helped give me the structure and laughter I needed. Thank you for your endless hours of support and direction.

To Bebe Coker, who, while everyone told me that I should sing, encouraged me to utilize the power of spoken words, thoughts, and dreams, thank you.

And I acknowledge you the reader for daring to be informed when it is so easy to do nothing at all.

Contents

I'M ON MY WAY
BUT YOUR FOOT
IS ON MY HEAD

Foreword

I've just moved to San Diego. Outside my window are mountains, trees, and birds I've never seen before. Every morning I give praise for this environment. I still can't believe that I live here. I moved here for work, family, and balance. Two out of three ain't bad. Los Angeles is close enough that I can drive there, where I'll be taping a new television series and hoping to start development on two—no, make that three—more.

I've only been back home a few hours. Yesterday I was in Virginia, and the day before that New York. Comedy appearances and lectures. In a few hours I'll be going to Western Night at my nephew William's school. Everyone else will be dressed like cowboys, but we're going as Cherokee Indians.

There are countless phone calls to return, agents and producers, professors and reporters. Have I really only been gone two days? I'll have to find out if my four-year-old nephew, Jabril, has stopped raiding the refrigerator in the middle of the night, and whether my two-year-old niece, Fatima, is over her ear infection.

I really have to get moving on my one-woman stage show, and meanwhile, I need to find a new nanny so my sister Chris can go back to her life in Chicago. Though it wouldn't be so bad if she decided to join me out here, my sister-friend . . .

My plate is full, but my cup runneth over. Life is a whirl of hopes and responsibilities, chores and possibilities. Sometimes it tires me out, but I rise to the occasion. I think.

I know that I've been fortunate. I've learned my lessons in the right order and I remember them.

Is there an order to the lessons of life? I think there is. I believe that we each have to pay attention to what we *need* in this life before we try to go after what we want. I believe that if we surround ourselves with stuff we don't need, the things that we do need will never reach us.

I'll never stop learning the lessons of my life. God is constantly reminding me of how little I know. A few months ago She sent me a dream, a dream that I think illustrates this perfectly:

Once there was a village of wishful children. They wished that they could crawl, and with much effort they did. They wished to walk, and they did. Then came running and dancing, and they did these things, but they wanted more. So they wished they could fly.

One of the children said, "But this is not within our power. We must wait as our parents do. We will fly just as they will someday, but it's not our time."

Then another child, one who was very lazy and yet very convincing, proclaimed, "I will not wait. Look at how old our parents are; they think they know everything, but they can't fly. I am not old, I have not waited, and I will not work. But I know how we can fly."

It was then that the children decided to go to the dream merchant. They knew that if they found him, he would have to grant their wish. (Children are often good at finding things because it is usually a child or childlike spirit that lost the thing in the first place.) They danced and sang and went looking for the dream merchant. And they found him.

When they did, they told him their desire. "We wish to fly, high above the birds, above the clouds. We want to fly."

The dream merchant sneered at the children. "Go away. Come back when you are old and you have done something in life. Come back when you're an ancestor."

But the children protested. "We want to fly now and you must give us this wish. We found you and you must."

The dream merchant thought for a second and then gave in, as he knew he had to. "All right, but since this is not a normal desire, it will cost you something—it will cost you your legs."

And now the children thought. "We need our legs," said one. "But we need to fly more," said the lazy one. "And when we fly, we have no need for legs."

"So off with our legs," the children said, laughing. And off they went.

The children did fly, high above the buildings and trees and above the clouds. It was a most incredible experience, more wonderful than any they had ever had. But as they were children, they hadn't had many experiences, so flying didn't mean that much to them and they grew tired of it quickly.

"We should go down now and play some other games, like kickball and kick-the-can," said one. But when they tried to land, they realized it was impossible to do without legs. They tried and tried, but couldn't do it. They began to yell for their parents.

The parents were confused when they saw their children. "What are you doing up there? Come down right now. You should not be flying; there is still much to learn."

"We can't," the children cried. "We have no legs. Please find the dream merchant."

When the parents heard this, they began to tear out their hair and wail as if someone had died. They knew that if the dream merchant was involved, something terrible would ensue.

Following the children's directions, the parents found the dream merchant. When the children saw him, they cried, "Please give us back our legs. You knew this was a trick. We are bored and tired and we want to land."

"I can't," the dream merchant said. "I must have forgotten to tell you and you never thought to ask. I can grant any wish, but I can't take one back."

"We want to land," the children cried again. But the dream merchant looked at them and then at their parents and said, "I'm sorry. This is what happens when you trade simple things that can take you everywhere for incredible things that take you only in circles."

With this the parents knew they had lost their children, and the children knew they had lost their childhood.

Next time you see a flock of birds that seem misdirected and cannot land, remember the children who refused to work for their dreams.

CHAPTER ONE

Getting to Know Me

Hi, my name is Bertice Berry. I know, you're thinking that I look like that other Black woman with dreadlocks. She's beautiful, but I'm not her. All Black women do not look alike.

The other day I got on the bus and this woman said, "You look just like Whoopi Goldberg."

I told her, "You're fat and White, but you don't look like Mama Cass."

I was poor, I was Black, and I was female. It seemed that everything outside of me said that I couldn't make it. But the tiny voice within said that I would.

I was born just in time to witness the life and death of John F. Kennedy, Martin Luther King Jr., and Malcolm X. The rise of rock and roll and the fall of George Wallace, only to see him rise again. I experienced the Motown sound the first time around, platform shoes, and mood rings. The singing of Mahalia Jackson, the Staple Sisters, Little Richard, and, oh, yeah, Elvis.

I remember when *colored* was the appropriate term and *Black* was derogatory—except in my house. "What color was the person colored?" my mother would always ask. I grew up with the Jackson 5, the Osmond Brothers, the King Family, Shaft—he's a bad mother, shut your mouth—Superfly, and Cleopatra Jones.

I had role models like Christie Love—stop right there, sugar—Julia, Eddie's father, and *The Undersea World of Jacques Cousteau*. (Did you know that he had a Black assistant? Child, they all do.)

It was a time when childhood rhymes were political chants: "'Ngawa, 'ngawa . . . this is Black Power. White boy, destroyed. I said it. I meant it. And I'm here to represent it." But still, love conquered all. It reigned supreme.

We all gathered around our TV sets when the Supremes showed America the beauty of Black women on *The Ed Sullivan Show*. Little Stevie, the Wonder, amazed us all. Jackie O. sported those pillbox hats and taught the country refinement, while my girl Angela Davis showed me what I wanted my Afro to look like and just how defiant a "lady" should be. Skirts were short and the summers seemed real long. Jesus moved to Haight-Ashbury. Conflict grew into war and White folks could now feel oppressed, too.

It was a time of confusion and revolution in the United States. It was a time of contradictions. It was a time when the nation saw its share of pure rage and hatred and, at the same time, felt a sense of resourcefulness and hope.

I am a product of that time. I am a combination of everything and everyone with whom I've come in contact: the words of Dr. Seuss and the ramblings of Dr. Spock. The brilliance of James Baldwin and the depth of Alice Walker. I'm spiritually moved by the music of Andrae Crouch and Oleta Adams makes me cry. I'll never chew with my mouth open, I know not to buy a pig in a poke, and I will never, ever forget where I've come from.

Every book I've ever read, every song I've ever heard, every word ever spoken to me have had influence, good and bad. Sometimes what's intended to be bad can turn out to be good. Like my childhood. It wasn't what my mother meant for me and certainly not what I want for my children. But here I am.

The Truth Is in the Details

We might as well get this over with. My name is Bertice. Two simple syllables: *Ber-tice*.

It isn't Bertrice, Bernice, Buttice, Patrice, or Erbrese. It seems like everybody from people who stop me in airports to get my autograph to Hollywood executives has a mental block about my name. I've sat through entire conversations being called everything from Burmese to Vertidal. It's not like my name is Sheilaquanda, though I do believe at times that Sheilaquanda is my alter ego.

When you go through life with a name that's unusual, it teaches you something. At first you suspect that a lot of folks don't have enough sense to wash the wax out of their ears. Eventually it dawns on you that a lot of people in this world don't truly listen. They hear something or see something, and instead of paying real attention to it, they label it as something they *think* they already know.

For instance: My mother was a single African-American woman raising seven kids with little income and even less opportunity. During my childhood, she became an abusive alcoholic.

Now stop right there, sugar. Up in your mind a tape is beginning to play that tells you, "Oh, yeah, I know what *that* means. She's Black and she was poor. *Swing low.* She's gonna be angry, and she—"

But that's someone else's movie. There's more to my life than that. Yes, we did have a hard time, and, yes, I have a lot of anger. But you have to work hard at getting me angry. Or you have to be a politician and not work at all. Just watch out when I start to move my neck.

There's more to my story than the poor, Black girl from the projects. I am also the first person in my family to attend, let alone graduate from, college, and I went on from there to get a Ph.D. in sociology. (So if you can't manage Bertice, think of me as Dr. Berry.) I spent a year as the host of my own nationally syndicated talk show, and I am a stand-up comic who's funny without ever talking about somebody else's mother or how I "do it."

Along the way, I've been a janitor, a bingo-caller, and I worked in a shelter for battered women. I've been a post office employee, a food-stamp bureaucrat, a teacher, and amicably divorced. I am also a single mother. There you go again with that moving picture of dirty children and a tired, sex-crazed woman in a food-stamp line. That movie was written by folks who don't know me or any other real people. They are the scriptwriters who use words like *jive* and *hip* and call women "Sweet Mammy." Please, who talks like that?

In actuality I've never had children of my own. I'm raising my sister's three children and we don't qualify for food stamps. But if we did, I wouldn't be embarrassed to use them.

There's a lot more to my experience than anything that tape in your head will tell you. I'm sure that there are folks who have done what I've done and who have been through what I've been through. But not all at once and not in one lifetime.

Or maybe there have been and I'm the only one who's still running around loose.

I'm on My Way, but Your Foot Is on My Head

This book is the story of the paths I've taken and those I'm still trying to avoid. Much of my life has been an obstacle course. I've been trying to break the cycles of poverty and abuse, while a whole group of spectators who couldn't jump off a curb if they tried have been yelling, "That girl is gonna fall flat on her big behind."

Sometimes I do fall, but thank God for that glorious cushion.

No matter where I go or what I do, there has always been someone yelling, "That's impossible!" or "Why give up everything you've done already for a chance on something you're not sure of?" Throughout my childhood, my education, and my professional life, I've left these naysayers behind. I had to, just like anyone who wants to make it. But they have played a part in my life.

There have also been people along the way yelling, "Go, girl. You can walk that walk." These people taught me to have faith in myself and God, to work hard, and to live my dreams. That's why I was able to break away from the cycles of doubt and discouragement.

Everybody who comes into this world gets caught up in the cycles that the people around them are fighting. There's no way you can avoid dealing with the problems that your parents and family have probably inherited from their parents and family.

But I know that you don't have to spend your life trapped in those cycles. You can finish them and move forward. You may even find other people following you—and the little child shall lead them.

This isn't about denying your past, about cutting yourself off from your culture and your people, pretending that they have nothing to do with you. You have to embrace those things, get to know them and understand them, wring everything you can that's good out of them. Then you have to honor them and share them with others.

There's a song I remember from church that says don't forget to remember where all your blessings come from. In that song it talks about remembering, recalling, and recollecting not only this life, but past lives and the experiences of those who have gone before.

Remembering that many of my ancestors were slaves, some of whom were killed because they wanted to read, remembering that I have done things they could never have imagined, remembering that my mother worked as hard as she could to put food on the table, remembering that someone who didn't even know me was willing to help me get an education—this helps keep me grounded. It helps me to stay true to what I believe, and it helps me to focus on what I need to do and how I need to get there.

Changing the Tapes

No matter how positive you try to be, things happen. And they will make you angry. This is dangerous because I often get the urge to slap somebody silly, and I don't have some device in my head that says, Yo, Bertice, chill. Don't do that. So I have to use humor when things make me angry. So far, it's worked, but I keep Johnnie Cochran's phone number by my bedside.

A lot of comedy comes from conversations I have with myself about all the things in the world that make me angry or despairing. I try to find the irony in life. Alice Walker has said there's a point at which even grief becomes absurd. At that point laughter gushes up to retrieve the sanity. I cultivate that laughter. My humor is not based on hatred; it comes from realizing how stupid other people can be. Not stupid as in Forrest Gump (by the way, didn't it bother anyone else that he was named after the founder of the Ku Klux Klan?). But stupid as in they haven't read a book in years or talked to anyone who's life doesn't revolve around soap operas or get his news from talk shows.

Herein lies the possibility to create change.

Now, I usually fly first-class, not because I have a lot of money, but because I fly so often to comedy gigs that I can get upgraded for free. Once when I had just taken a seat on a plane, the flight attendant came up to me and said, "You must be in the wrong seat. Somebody named *Doctor* Berry is supposed to be sitting there." I took a deep breath and fought back the urge to punch her in her implants.

I pursed my lips and batted my eyes and said, "Oh, I can understand your mistake. It's because I look so—young." Girlfriend spent the whole flight trying to give me every peanut on the plane.

If you hear about racism in one of those serious, angry discussions Americans love to have, you're going to come away with one of two responses. You'll either say, "Like, that happened two hundred years ago. It wasn't me, leave me alone." Or you'll say, "That's right, you the enemy. I'm gonna kill you today."

The great thing about humor is that it really does have a lasting impression. Right now, if I told you a joke about a poodle, I could make you laugh. A few months from now, if you saw a poodle, you'd snicker. You might not remember the joke, and you probably wouldn't remember where you heard it. But you'd associate that poodle with the emotion it evoked.

By changing the emotions that are evoked, my humor tries to interrupt the tapes in people's heads, the tapes that say that Asians are bad drivers, that African-Americans have rhythm while Whites don't have any. Actually, they do, it's just on the wrong beat. Irish are drunks, and White people smell like dogs when they get wet. Hah! Now most Whites probably never heard that one. But the next time it rains, they'll be checking.

A young woman once told me, "Jehovah's Witnesses steal."

I really had to say, "Whaaaat?" 'cause in my whole life I had never heard this. I asked her why she thought this, and she said, "Well, when they come to your house, you have to turn out all the lights and hide until they go away."

Nobody ever told her this, but she believed it because of her parents' behavior. It was the only way she could make sense of what happened. All right, it wasn't the only way, but she never stopped to think about a new reason once she'd figured this one out.

That's the power of what you hear about yourself and other people—it keeps reinforcing itself unless you stop it. Even if you think it's not true, you're still going to wonder the next time the tape starts to run in your head.

I was poor, I was Black, and I was female. It seemed that everything outside of me said that I couldn't make it. But the tiny voice within said that I would.

I'll always remember a character from the Li'l Abner comic strip, Joe *\@#/?. He's the one who was always walking around with the rain cloud over his head. Other people would be standing in the sun, but Joe *\@#/? lived in a perpetual downpour. "We'll never make it" was his trademark whine.

If I wanted to live that way, I could have my own personal hurricane.

My own mother was the first to tell me I'd never amount to anything. She would curse the day I was born. Then, in the same breath, she'd cry and pray for my success. That was the mother I chose to listen to, a woman who believed that there was a way out, even if she'd lost sight of it.

Other people took up the refrain that I'd never make it. When I said that I wanted to go to college, one of my high school teachers predicted that I'd never be accepted, and if by some fluke I did get in, I shouldn't unpack because surely they'd be sending me home.

I lived out of my suitcase for the first five weeks of college. And even once I realized I wasn't the victim of some big practical joke, I still worried about making it. Of course, I did graduate and I did get the President's Cup for Most Outstanding Student. And it was presented to me by a two-time Nobel Prize–winner, Linus Pauling. *And* then there is the matter of the master's degree and the Ph.D., thank you very much, Mr. High School Teacher. Nah, nah nah nah nah, nah.

All my life I heard that if I walked like, talked like, dressed like, ate like, acted like, and—most important—looked like the people in charge, I would be accepted. I would be, I would be . . . a Huxtable. But I realized that I am never going to look like a White man. Thank you, Jesus.

It's not that there's something wrong with looking like a White man. Some of my best friends are White men. But I am a Black woman, and that gives me a beauty and a strength that is unique. We possess a quality that cannot be captured or copied. Sure, plenty of folks are trying to suck our flavor, as the young people say. But all the collagen injections in the world can't give you the kiss of a Black woman's lips.

There is a lot of power in being a Black woman, but most of the world still thinks like James Brown when he sings that song, "It's a Man's World." So, as good as I am, I'm probably just getting up to about 10 percent of my potential.

Finding the Power

People say, "Stop and smell the roses." I say, "Take time out to dream."

If you dream something, you can think of a way to make it happen. It takes work, but it's the only way to erase that tape in your head that says, "You'll never make it." Dreaming about a better life was the way that I started to break free of the cycles that had gripped my family for generations.

Once I had a dream, I could imagine living a life that was free of bitterness, powerlessness, and fear. I could define that life, figure out what I would have to do to get there, and then start working toward it.

It started with college. I began dreaming of going to college at a point when I often had to do my homework by candle-light because we didn't have the money to pay the electric bill. I had no idea how I'd afford to go, but I worked my hair off to be a good student. I found other people who believed that I could do it—in fact, I found people who were more certain than I was—and they helped me apply. Thanks to the generosity of a benefactor I'll always love and respect, I was able to afford to go.

I kept on dreaming of new things I could do with my education. And when the chance came along to start doing stand-up comedy, I was ready to leave the academic world behind, despite the fact that my family, which had just figured out why I'd spent all those years in school, thought I was crazy.

Maybe I was crazy, too, when I agreed to do *The Bertice Berry Show.* I sure considered the possibility during the grueling, heartbreaking days when we'd shoot sometimes three shows back-to-back. I wondered even more when I had to deal with Hollywood hotshots.

But you know, I don't think I made any mistakes, at least not about those choices. I've got plenty of other things to regret. But dreaming isn't one of them.

Plenty of people dream, but they never do anything about

making their dreams real. Their dreams are all about what life will be like when everything is good, but they never include the stuff in between the good and the bad.

Other people work hard, but they work just to get by, to pay the bills or keep somebody off their back. Those people are only working for someone else. They never work for themselves because they don't have a dream behind all their labor.

I believe that dreaming is more natural and realistic than doing all the things that people say you're supposed to do. Whenever I think of people who have told me to stop dreaming, my neck starts to move.

What makes dreaming and working pay off is faith. Faith allows us to take risks, to go ahead when other people, people who are close to us, people who are *supposed* to support us, say, "Why you wanna give up a good-paying job to be a stand-up comic?"

Because I like to laugh, and if I'm working a job that I don't like, it just won't be funny.

The Way Out

Like I said, life is full of cycles. The cycles of your own life are always connected to someone else's. Your parents were running a relay 'round a track, and when you came along, they passed you the baton. You never really got to ask if this was your race. You never asked, "What's this for? Why am I running?" And if you did, they would have said what their parents said to them: "Because I told you to." The pressure to keep going in the same direction, as fast as possible, is intense.

Yet when you dream, you get to have a choice. In a dreamworld you paint a picture of reality. You can make anything happen. When I was a girl, I had horrible nightmares. I dreamt of giant bill collectors and this beast called The Man. They would attack my family and keep us from escaping the Land of Poverty.

One night I decided to fight back. I could hardly wait to go to sleep. When I did, they were waiting for me. I told them that I had the power to become anything. And so I did. But no matter what I became, they tracked me down. Eventually I learned how to disappear. I would actually open my eyes, come out of the dream, close them, and go back into it. When I did this, The Man and his cronies realized my power and left me alone.

I began to use the dream-gift to see whatever I wanted and to go anywhere in my dreams. I read about Africa and I'd go there. I heard about Martinique and I'd go there, too. Then I decided that my dreams could become reality.

When you have faith in yourself and your dream, you can head off in a new direction, leaving that racetrack behind. Some of the spectators may boo and hiss. Some of them may cheer. Someone else caught up in the same race may try to trip you. But, baby, you can still crawl.

Learning to keep moving despite my fears and the naysayers was perfect training for the comedy circuit. The very first gig I had was in Cuyahoga Falls, Ohio. We called it Caucasian Falls because it's got a lot of 'em.

In my first routine I started out as Tina Turner. I had this big, cheap wig I'd almost had to fight a transvestite hooker for in the wig shop. I put it on, ran out onstage, and started a hilarious imitation of Tina. The audience roared.

Then every word I'd ever heard from some doubting Thomas rushed back into my head. They're not going to like this, I said to myself. Right when I did, I opened the door to doubt and I closed the door on my abilities. I forgot the rest of the words to the song I was singing.

I froze. The audience sat there waiting for the next line they knew had to be coming. I didn't have one, but I had to do something. I turned up my nose and opened my mouth like I'd seen Tina do. The crowd roared again. Think fast, Bertice.

"You ever wonder why Tina always looks like this?" I asked. "Because she smells something. There's a guy in the front row at all her concerts," I said real slow as if I were about to introduce "Proud Mary," "whose job, his only job, is to pass gas."

The crowd went into hysterics and I was in. The Caucasians of Caucasian Falls loved me, and I was still very Black and proud.

So whenever I hear those people who are screaming, "No!" I know to do whatever it takes to drown them out.

Question: What Are You Going to Be When You Grow Up? Answer: You Mean I Have a Choice?

If you had a choice, what would you have been? I mean, truly? There's no way of knowing for sure. If, as a child, I had been exposed to all of the information and ideas I have now, would I have gone off in the same direction? In my miseducation, I had to come up with all kinds of ways to deal with messages that said that I was too fat, too ugly, too Black. I learned to be popular by being smart and funny. My dreams and the paths I've taken were shaped by the choices I didn't have, but look where they've gotten me.

When I was in high school, my family's finances hit an all-time low and we were evicted from our house. We were so broke that we couldn't afford to pay anybody to move us. We took only what we could carry.

I had only a few clothes to carry, so I managed to salvage an old cardboard-covered record player and two albums: Patti LaBelle and Phoebe Snow. In the temporary housing unit we moved into, I played those albums loud and I sang them even louder. Luckily, the housing shelter had walls made of cinder block, so no one could hear me.

The place was cold and desolate, and I'm sure that this was done deliberately. The designers wanted to make sure that each temporary family would get out quickly so the next poor family could move in. The cinder block kept us from doing anything even halfway permanent, like hanging a picture.

I'd sit on the cement floors, staring at the bare walls and Patti LaBelle's album cover. Phoebe's album cover was nice, but it was a little girl on a dirt road, and that was where I was coming from. Patti's cover had her all made up and sitting at a table in a fine restaurant. There was a man in the picture, but she was the star. That was where I was going. I was sure of it. I sang with the album and vowed that when I grew up, I wouldn't be poor and that I'd always pay my bills on time. I was gonna be somebody and I would even meet Patti LaBelle. I'd talk to her, thank her for this inspiration.

After I had made it as a comic and a talk-show host, I went to a Patti LaBelle concert. I was sitting in the front row when she broke into one of the songs from the album. I started crying and I didn't know why. Suddenly it all came back. I saw the cinder-block walls and the beautiful album cover.

My friend, the actor T. C. Carson, was there and held me. He looked at me and said, "I hope these are happy tears because your mascara's running."

After the concert I went backstage to meet Patti. When she saw me, she gave me a big old sistergirl hug and handed me an armful of her roses. I thanked her for helping me dream.

If I hadn't dreamed, I couldn't have been in the front row of that concert. You can't choose a path through life without a dream. And the dream's gotta be bigger than the world around you. If the only successful people children see are drug dealers, that's what they'll aspire to be. Quick, call Newt Gingrich. The government can now stop funding research to find out why Willie becomes a drug dealer.

Most people are so accustomed to not having a choice that they don't even notice. Being a Black woman, I recognize this oppression on at least two counts. This is not to say that all Whites and men are completely free to choose either; God knows, there are some who should be making other choices.

This sense that somebody is trying to limit my choices is often the source of my anger. There's an old saying that if you make a woman mad, you'd better sleep with one eye open. Well, if you try to take away my choices, you'd better not go to sleep at all.

People often say that Black women have attitudes. Everybody does, but the term takes on a negative connotation whenever it's used about me and mine. Our hands start to fly, usually landing on our hips, and then our necks start to move. When folks ask me what the neck-moving business is all about, I explain—in the kindest way possible, of course—that my neck is attached to my last and final nerve and that somebody, usually the person I'm speaking to, has just leaned on it.

If you don't want to hear me sing, don't pull my string.

Sometimes it isn't other people or society that is holding us back. We can have clear opportunities and choices but won't take them. Instead, we keep running around the same track, holding on to the same baton, because it's what we know and anything else is just too scary.

I know that sometimes I have delayed my journey because

I've been spending too much time trying to prove all the naysayers wrong. I've been too worried about whether or not people would like me. It was time I wasted, plain and simple.

Making your journey—free from everybody else's ideas about where you should go—is the reason you've been put on this earth. But it's easy to get lost. When that happens, the best thing you can do is look for the place where you started. Then you know what you're leaving behind.

Where I'm Coming From

Mrs. Closson was giving us her daily geography lesson. Today, like all others, the class got to participate. Our second-grade teacher wanted to know whose family had come from the farthest distance.

Each child got up and went to the map. Andre Perry said his people were from Maryland. Someone else said Pennsylvania. Most of the kids said Delaware. One kid stood up and said, "We're from Florida." I knew this was not the truth. I had overheard the adults talking one day; they said that as far back as they could remember, everyone in his family had been born in the state penitentiary. I wanted to tell on him, but I just rolled my eyes.

I was last and this was unusual. I was an eager learner, always the first to wave my entire arm. By this time the class was looking at me and so was Mrs. Closson.

"Where are you from, Bertice?" she asked.

I wanted to name some faraway place and beat the rest of the class at this game. But I couldn't. I really didn't know where my family was from, and I wasn't allowed to tell lies. We weren't even allowed to say the word lie. *We had to say things like, "Mom, Kevin told a story."*

So I sat there with no answer. I loved Mrs. Closson and I wanted to please her. But I had no response. Then, as if struck by lightning, I had the answer. I could tell the truth and be unique at the same time.

I stood up, but did not go the map.

"My answer's not even up there," I proclaimed.

"Oh, no?" Mrs. Closson asked as her eyebrows went up.

Her map was of the United States and she probably thought that I'd indicate that my people were from Africa. I wish that I had thought of that. Surely it would have made that dashiki-Afro-wearing-say-it-loud-I'm-Black-and-I'm-proud woman very happy. But nope, my answer was not that clever. Yet it was the truth and it was funny.

"I come from my mother."

The whole class broke into laughter. Kids were rolling on their sides. Mrs. Closson had to slap her ruler on the chalkboard to restore order. "Sit down, Miss Berry," she said. She was angry.

But I was right. I had come from a far distance. I had come from my mother, who had come from hers. And the journey was long and tiresome.

Much of what I know about my mother and my family I only learned when I started to write this book. When I ask my mother and my older sister Chris why they never talked about the past, they say because I never asked. My time was spent coping with the daily task of trying not to make them any more angry than they already were and dreaming of my own escape. If only I had known the truth sooner.

When I was a kid and read *Macbeth,* I realized that if you knew enough about people's background, you could never hate them. All you could do was understand. Macbeth is a murderer, but because you know some of what he's been through, you feel sorry for him. I started calling this my "Macbeth principle"—and I used it to understand my mother's bouts of rage.

Because the women in my family have had their children

late in life, I only have to go back three generations to find my enslaved ancestors. My great-grandmother Annie Paskins was born a slave and lived on the Hunn family farm near Lebanon, Delaware, just south of Dover. Yes, children, Delaware was a slave state.

Annie was only half-Black. My family doesn't know who her father was; they say she wouldn't talk about it. But since she was also half-White, it was assumed that her father was one of her owner's people.

After slavery was abolished, Annie was forced to stay with the Hunns. Many supposedly free Black people were intimidated or lied to in order to keep them doing the same work they'd done before. The abolition of slavery meant nothing to Annie until she met John Henry Freeman. He married her and managed to get her away from the Hunns. They set up as sharecroppers near Lebanon and eventually owned their own tiny parcel they called a farm.

John Henry was not African-American. He was full-blooded Cherokee. My mother remembers him as a regal-looking man with long, coal-black braids. He identified with and loved Black folks. He named himself after the folk hero who worked on the railroads and was so strong he could out-work a steam drill. He took the last name Freeman so that everyone would know that he was just that, a free man.

John Henry's strength was not physical but emotional and spiritual. He was a calm and peaceful man, and it was a good thing, because for most of her life, Annie was not that kind of person.

Annie's hopes of finally finding real freedom with John Henry were destroyed by the realities of jim crow and poverty. She became an angry and bitter woman. Maybe because she wanted to escape her mother's fury, Annie's daughter Caroline became pregnant. But the father—my grandfather—didn't stay, and my mother was left to be raised by Annie and John Henry.

Caroline spent most of her time working for a White family somewhere in Pennsylvania. She only made it home to see my mother, Beatrice, at best once a month; usually it was a lot less. That left my mother to stand in as Annie's whipping post. John Henry was her only comfort. He held her when she cried, took her fishing, and stood between her and Annie's wrath at the world. Then he died when she was about ten.

When Caroline did make it home, things weren't any better for my mother. Caroline had all her mother's rage. To say that Caroline was an angry woman was like saying that getting hit by a car can hurt. Mom would retreat to the outhouse, the only place where she had some solitude and peace. Even that wasn't enough. One day Caroline decided that my mother had spent too long in the outhouse, so she set it on fire. With my mother inside.

My mother wore the hand-me-downs from the people that Caroline worked for. She never got anything that was too good. Her aunt and cousin would always select the better items from what Caroline had sent and leave the rest for Mom.

I used to think my mother was a selfish woman because whenever I'd buy presents or give money to people who'd been good to me, she'd get jealous. She'd go into fits about how I cared about others more than I cared about her. I understand her now. Somehow, I did then, too.

Caroline had three other children, and it became my mother's responsibility to take care of my aunts Catherine and Freda and my uncle Sonny. Before she knew it, her life was slipping away.

Like her mother, my mother tried to find freedom with a

man and she got pregnant. But it was no escape. To support herself and her child, my mother had to leave home and start working for a White family. It was the same cycle her mother had followed.

My eldest sibling, Myrna, was sent to live with her father's family. She always complained that my mother gave her away. This was part of Myrna's grief, something she held on to until she died.

But my mother kept looking for her own John Henry, a man with the ability to love and protect her. She had another child, my sister Christine, who was sent to live with Caroline. Eventually, there were five more children. It became Chris's job to care for us, so that she was repeating the cycle our mother had tried to flee, caring for children when she was just a child.

Who I Am

There's a sign over the freeway on the way into my childhood hometown that says, "Wilmington, Delaware, a place to be somebody." I don't know if that sign was there when I was growing up. It sure didn't feel like a place to be somebody, but it was home.

When I was four, we moved from the projects to Wilmington's East Side. Years before *The Jeffersons,* we were happy to be movin' on up. The projects were confined, designed like old slave quarters: low and close together so nobody could make a quick getaway. There was a real stigma to living there. Kids who lived just across the street, but not in the projects, would taunt us. "You live in the projects, you live in the projects." I didn't know why, but I hated hearing this.

And, hey, isn't a project like some kind of experiment and shouldn't somebody start working on phase two?

By this point my mother was working as a nurse's assistant in a nursing home. It was hard work and she was proud of it. She kept her uniform whiter than anything I ever saw. But because she was always on her feet, she got a terrible case of athlete's foot she couldn't cure. Her feet smelled like a line-backer's. To this day, the smell of bad feet reminds me of an overworked, underpaid woman in white.

Whenever my siblings and I played the dozens (that's just a friendly game of name-calling for those of you who may be culturally impaired), the smell of my mother's feet became the weapon of choice. We'd start out with minor insults like "You're so fat that pigs think you're their first cousin." (This was usually aimed at me.) We'd move up a notch to insults about one another's character: "You're so low you could play hardball with the curb."

Eventually, someone would get downright dirty: "So you smell like Mom's feet." Right there, in the midst of the hisses and the boos, the game would stop because there was no insult that could top that one.

Whenever my family made fun of our unfunny situation, we'd be less unhappy. We made light of the fact that at times we had no food or electricity. We'd ask my mother what was for dinner and she'd say, "Poke, rolls, and grits. Poke your mouth out, roll your eyes, and grit your teeth, 'cause that's all you're getting."

When we were able to laugh, the problems didn't seem so big. Real, yes, but not as big. The laughter was always effective. However, you can only laugh so long before the reality creeps back in.

Up until I was ten years old, my mother was a stable force

for our family. But as her body grew more tired, so did her spirit. She began to use alcohol as an escape; as she drank, her rage increased.

One day my mother came home completely tired and half-drunk from a stop she'd made on the way. That liquor store on the corner of Twenty-third and Market Street is still there, and back then it was one of the few places that would extend her credit. I wish they hadn't. It's funny how stuff you don't need always does good business. Like today's drugs, junk can always find a good corner.

After picking up a six-pack and a fifth of gin, my mother arrived home earlier than expected. We hadn't had time to go through the "quick, fix up the living room before Mom gets here" business. The house was a complete mess. Mom started yelling about how we were ungrateful and how she was sick and tired of us.

I must have been in the way or was looking too much like my father because she began to single me out. She told me that I'd never amount to anything and that I was a no-good, stupid bitch. Those words hurt more than twenty beatings. I wondered how and why she could be so cruel. I didn't know anything then about her past. I wish I had because I could have applied my Macbeth principle, which said as long as you knew why people were the way they were, you could forgive them for what they did.

Even though my mind didn't have a clue, my spirit did. Something within told me that my mother didn't mean the things she said and that our punishments were a result of her pain. Although I didn't know exactly the curse she felt pressing down on her, I swore on that day that I wouldn't repeat her life. I vowed to myself that I would never drink.

I also promised myself that day that I would never have

children. I was afraid that they would hold me back. Or, worse, that I would treat them like my mother treated me.

A Lifetime Occupation

In Her infinite wisdom, God has held me to my promises and has helped me keep them. I still don't drink or do drugs. Never have, never will. I'm a Black woman from the land of the free and the home of the brave. I don't need any more illusions.

But God has also given me the opportunity to do better than I believed I could, which is why I am now raising two nephews and a niece. With them I have the chance to break free of the cycles that my mother knew and to keep these kids from getting caught in them as well.

Desperation taught me to do everything I could to change the circumstances of my life. And from the need to laugh at the things that got me down, I learned to be funny. I can make money by making people laugh at their own stupid ideas. I've already got enough material to last a few centuries.

Right after I'd gotten my Ph.D., I was on a trip with some friends to celebrate. We pulled over to use the bathroom at a busy rest stop. When I came out of the stall, two women were waiting.

"You go first," one said to the other.

"No, you go. I insist," the other woman replied.

These women were afraid to use the toilet after a Black person! Here I was, *Dr. Berry,* and I still had to put up with these racist attitudes. I had done everything I was supposed to! But these women still couldn't see me as anything but some dark and scary monster.

It took some effort, but I didn't spit on them. Instead, I pulled the sleeves of my jacket down over my hands, real obviously, as I turned on the water faucet. And I called out to my friend Keisha, "Girl, be careful in here. You know White people got all kinds of diseases."

She laughed out loud and so did a few of the other women who were waiting. One woman touched me on the shoulder and said, "We're not all like that."

And I'm sure that now, wherever they are, every time they go to a public rest room, those two women are waving their arms and yelling, "Yo, Black lady, let me go after you."

Of course, some people need a lot more education. During the year that *The Bertice Berry Show* was on the air, we had all kinds of trouble with an executive who thought we were doing everything wrong. "I want to see chairs flying," he'd tell us; he thought the answer to ratings success was to start a fight. But I'm a lover, not a fighter.

I didn't want my nose broken and I didn't want one of my guests hunting another one down and blowing his brains out. I knew what kind of show I had signed on to do and I kept doing it.

Even after he knew that our show wasn't going to be renewed, this big shot kept after me to shave my hair off. (Excuse me, but don't they do that to people who are going to the chair?) Now, I've had dreadlocks since before they were fashionable. I like them. But this man decided that they were hurting our ratings. He called me into his office and told me that research showed that Black people didn't like my hair. Well, telling Bertice Berry, Ph.D., about research is like waving a red flag in front of a bull. You know I'm gonna charge.

It turned out that he didn't know much about this market research that had supposedly been done. He couldn't answer a single question I asked. Instead, he played me a tape of ten women being interviewed about my hair.

Just as if I were toothpaste, nine out of the ten women said they liked my hair, or at least, they liked it on me. But one woman in a weave—and a very bad weave—leaned forward and waved her hand in a ShaNayNay fashion and said, "I just don't like her hair. She need to get it did. I mean, why can't she wear a wig or somptang? Like, you know, she be embarrassing to Black people."

In *The Mis-Education of the Negro,* Carter G. Woodson wrote that Black people have been trained to use the back door for so long that they won't even think of using the front door. If a back door doesn't exist, they'll build one. Well, this woman was a carpenter.

You know I didn't shave my hair. I did a makeover show instead and put on all kinds of wigs and let the audience call in with their opinions. Some of them liked the wigs better. This is America, I expected it. Most of them, however, didn't.

After we knew we'd been canceled, the executive called to tell me not to worry, that we'd be successful in taking the show elsewhere but only if I shaved my hair. I asked him if he knew what he was saying. "The show's canceled," I said. "It's all over." Then I asked him to visualize something:

"Imagine this. We're in a big field. Oh, let's say it's a cotton field. It's hot and I'm picking cotton. Lots of it. And you're up on this horse. You're cracking a whip and telling me to pick more cotton. But there's a problem. The problem is that it's *my* field, and you are only a sharecropper."

He told me that, after I calmed down, I should think about it. He's still waiting.

When the first verdict came down that cleared those Los Angeles police officers who'd beaten Rodney King, I was on a comedy tour. I was enraged. I tried to riot, but I was in upstate New York and I couldn't find five other Black people.

Instead, I went to the mall. I knew I had to find somebody to talk to about this disgrace. My American heritage was infuriated, but it was my African heritage that reminded me, No, try love first. So I started talking to people at the mall. Clerks would say, "How are you today?" I'd reply, "I am really upset about this Rodney King thing."

And they would say, *"Me, too!"* Right there in the middle of the mall, we had discussion groups, talking about why we were mad, what we could do about it, whom we could write and call. Black people, White people, Asians, Hispanics, we found out that we shared a sense of justice and a love of society, despite its failings.

(You know the other great thing? I got 15 percent off everything. No lie. People were feeling guilty and I said, "Okay.")

I believe that the real hope for change in this country lies in the everyday people who do everyday things to confront hatred, to learn more about each other and to erase the tapes in their heads.

The wonderful thing is that those efforts aren't just good for our society, they're fantastic steps for anyone who takes them. They teach you new things. They make you question your stereotypes about others and yourself. They help you learn from people you would never have known if you hadn't been willing to ask some questions and *listen to the answers.* Doing this won't make you any less Black or White or anything else. It will only make you more human.

Once you begin to educate yourself, you'll find that your understanding of the world is amplified. New possibilities will open up for you. You'll have new choices, whole new ways to dream that you could never have imagined before.

All of a sudden you're not only breaking cycles, you're creating a whole new path. And the next thing you know, people are following *you*. There's no telling where that kind of path can take you.

CHAPTER TWO

Magic and Motherhood

I never really wanted children. But then I thought I did but I was running out of time. My biological clock had gone off but I didn't know it. It was digital and I couldn't hear it ticking. One night it got unplugged and it's been flashing midnight ever since.

*M*y mother had supernatural powers a long time before Dionne Warwick got lost on the way to San Jose and stumbled across her psychic friends. (But, God, that woman can sing.) My mother had eyes in the back of her head and could hear a rat piss on cotton, as she often told us. I've inherited her abilities; it just took me a long time to learn how to use them.

At night my brothers and sisters and I would be in our beds whispering about how much our mother got on our nerves. "She makes me sick."

"Me, too!"

"I can't wait until I'm grown so I can get out of here!"

Then a shadow would appear in our doorway and answer back, "I can't wait either."

So now, half an hour after bedtime, I can stand in the hallway of my own house and shout, "Go to sleep," and I know that the kids I'm raising are talking about me and how I drive them crazy. I can ask who sneaked food out of the freezer in the middle of the night, or who forgot to shut the door behind them, *and I'll know the answer.*

But back in my childhood, I didn't understand how my

mother knew all she knew. She would sneak into our lives as if she were Angelique from *Dark Shadows,* uttering some grave prophecy. She told me that I should never have children. Instead, I should see the world and live the life we had stolen from her. When she'd whisper, "Don't ever have children, don't let them tie you down," it was as if she could see into the future when I'd be raising three kids and they'd be whispering about me.

But I'm getting ahead of my story. Before I tell you about being a mother, I need to tell you about being a child.

On Gordon Street

The house my mother was so happy to move into was on Gordon Street. It would still hold my brightest revelations and darkest fears if it hadn't been torn down.

Gordon Street was not really a street; it was an alley wedged between Twenty-second and Twenty-third Streets. There were only two houses on the entire block. The rest of the street was lined with lime-green garages; lime-green—the color of bad polyester clothes and limes. People would store old cars there, or anything else that didn't fit into their lives. But for us, it wasn't the projects, it was progress.

At the end of the block was a much bigger garage that stored something far more dreadful than some beat-up old cars. It was the clubhouse for Delaware's very own all-Black motorcycle gang, the Thunderguards.

They were aptly named. Gordon Street echoed with the sound of motorcycles day and night. Vroom! Vroom! Vroom! The rhythm of our lives adjusted to fit the noise; we could break off a conversation right in the middle as a squad of

Thunderguards rode by, then pick up again as soon as it was possible to be heard.

When I took a job teaching in the Virgin Islands, people warned me that the college was right next to the airport. It would take months, they predicted, before I adjusted to the roar of the jets. If they hadn't said anything, I would never have noticed. Airplane pilots don't try to impress each other with the roar of their engines.

Still, my mother was convinced we had made a step up in that house. The yard was a dirt field with a tree and a wooden fence. The house had three bedrooms, a dining room, a basement and an attic, and a front porch. More than what most people could hope for, she told us.

At a time when most Americans were excited about the coming of electric heat, we were still two steps behind with our coal furnace. In the center of our front porch was a coal shoot. We'd get all excited when the coal man would come. He would back his truck up to our porch and drop the load of black coal down the shoot to our basement. We'd run back and forth from the basement to the porch yelling, "Here it comes y'all, here it comes!" We couldn't always afford to buy coal.

In a way that furnace was a lucky thing, because when we'd run out of what coal we could afford and my brothers had snuck everything they could out from under the fence at the coal yard, we could always go on a hunt for pieces of old furniture the neighbors had thrown out. If we couldn't find any, we'd use our own.

My mother would put whatever we could find into that furnace. One of her true talents was building a fire. She'd toss large chunks of wood into that furnace with one hand and with the other poke them down with a long iron rod. People would say, "That Bea can bank a fire," as if she were making biscuits or something. She did what she could to keep us warm. Sometimes she couldn't.

Airing My Mother's Dirty Laundry

Opposite the furnace in the basement was my mother's best friend: her washing machine. Like the furnace, it was out-dated, a wringer model, but it got the job done. As soon as my mother got home from work, she'd go to the basement to wash the mounds of clothes that would never quite disappear. We used to say that washing clothes was my mother's hobby.

The basement was her place for solitude and refuge, like that outhouse had been until Caroline set it on fire. Mom would go downstairs with a six-pack of beer, some gin, her cigarettes, and a heart full of pain. She'd get drunk, wash clothes, and talk to God. *Lord, why do I have children who just won't listen? Why are their clothes so goddamned dirty? Excuse me for cursing, God, but when am I going to get a break?*

My own performances now don't require the six-pack, the gin, or the cigarettes, but I understand the lament, even if what I need isn't a break so much as an increase in patience and understanding. Scratch that. I don't need patience and understanding, I need kids who listen. Lord knows that children can be a trial, and no matter what you try to tell them, they have to learn a lot of it for themselves.

We were never allowed to go near my mother's washing machine. It was the one thing she called her own. So of course that meant the time would come when I had to discover what made that machine so sacred. When I was five years old, my wonder about the appeal of the washing machine was out of control.

My brother Kevin was my best friend. He is less than a year older than me; growing up, we did everything together. We'd once heard our mother say we used toilet paper like it was water. So we decided to wash some toilet paper and hang it out to dry. Who says poor people don't recycle?

We decided to start with clean toilet paper. Kevin gathered all that he could find. Then he fed it into the wringer, by far the most interesting part of the machine. The toilet paper got all clumped up and we knew that something was wrong. Kevin and I stared at each other, thinking the same thing: Oooh, you're going to get it.

"You better get that paper out or you're going to be in trouble," Kevin said.

"You put it in, so you get it out," I told him.

"You get it out."

"No, you get it out."

"I'm going to tell Mom you put it in there."

Now, even though it was a forbidden act in our house, Kevin could lie. Whenever he was in trouble, he would stop and say, "Let me think of a lie now." We used to call him Lie-lac.

He finally convinced me that since he was the oldest, Mom would listen to him. I should have known better. My mother never took the word of one of her children against the other. She simply beat us all.

I tried to get the paper out, and the next thing I knew my arm was being crushed. Blood was everywhere. Kevin was screaming at the top of his lungs and my mother and my sister Chris came running. Mom called her sister Catherine to take us to the hospital, so I knew that this was serious; my mother never took any of us to the hospital.

I spent two weeks there waiting for surgery, but it turned

out I didn't need it because my arm had completely healed. Proof that God takes care of fools and babies.

I still get real sad when I think about the fact that my mother found friendship with a washing machine. That the only real relief she had was from washing other people's clothes. But after a long day with three kids, I find myself talking to the vacuum cleaner. It does what it's supposed to do, when it's supposed to do it, and it doesn't ask why. Nor does it complain that you just gave a Popsicle to the toaster.

Can't Function Without Dysfunction

The fact is that you can't choose your family. Even though a bunch of people with similar genes are thrown together in the same house, and they eat together, follow the same rules, and listen to the same music, they come out completely different. You have to learn to live with each one of them in a way that is unique.

Every family is dysfunctional, but believe me, my family was dysfunctional long before anybody even thought up the word.

We were never allowed to talk about our problems outside the home. My mother told us that if we did, people would come and take us away. This frightened me. I envisioned White people in suits packing us all up and taking us to some place out of Oliver Twist. Newt Gingrich would have been happy.

We couldn't talk about our problems when we were at home either. During those late-night sessions when we'd whisper about our mother, it was never more than a few minutes before we'd hear, "Shut up in there, I know you're talking about me." We were like the McLaughlin Group of the Ghetto: Everybody had something to say, and we said it, but no problems were solved and we never changed anything.

Looking back, it's possible for me to recognize incidents now that give me an insight I would have longed for then.

Once, my aunt Geraldine asked my mother if she could keep me. I heard the entire conversation through the screen door. Aunt Geraldine had four sons and no daughters. She loved me and told my mother that she would take good care of me, bringing me over for regular visits so that I wouldn't forget who my mother was.

I loved Aunt Geraldine. She thought I was pretty. "Who's the cutest girl in the projects?" she'd ask. I wondered whom she meant, since no one had ever called me cute—and we didn't live in the projects anymore. "Who's the cutest *redhead* girl in the projects?" she'd specify. "Oh, me," I'd answer, knowing that I was the only red-haired Black girl I'd ever seen.

Aunt Geraldine always had baked goodies—sweet-potato pie, bread pudding, cookies. Her house smelled like cinnamon and vanilla. I sat outside on those steps and prayed for my mother to say yes to Aunt Geraldine. But she didn't. She said that she had brought me into the world and she would get me through.

At the time, I thought my mother was being selfish. It didn't make any sense that she didn't want to lighten her load. She was constantly screaming at us. At times, she even threatened to leave us: "One of these days, you're going to miss me when I'm gone. I'm not coming back. You'll see."

I was torn whenever my mother said these things. Some days I'd pray that she'd never come home. But whenever she was late coming home from work, all of us kids would sit around the door frightened that she was making good on her word. And when we saw her coming around that corner, we'd go back to wishing she hadn't.

Now Aunt Geraldine was giving my mom an opportunity to ease her burden, and she wouldn't take it. I cried and cried, and every time my mother had one of her screaming fits, I would remember the offer my mother had refused.

Today I understand the importance of this Black woman's keeping her family together. My mother had been raised by a woman who could remember slavery. Our family history as slaves demanded that she do nothing less—my mother's whole sense of self depended on keeping her family whole.

That wholeness of family is one of the cycles I picked up from my mother. There were times in my life when I thought it was something that wasn't going to be my struggle, too, and I was determined to make sure that it wasn't. I was wrong.

I Got All My Sisters in Me

All my sisters have been caught up in that cycle in one way or another.

Myrna was the oldest of us, a beautiful, handsome woman. She had a mole on the tip of her nose, which she said made her a witch. If Myrna was a witch, she was a good one.

Myrna was raised mainly by her father's family. When she was in her twenties, she moved to New York. I loved getting her letters, scented with patchouli or lavender. She started them all the same way: "Dear Bessie, my beloved, most beautiful sister." (Bessie is my middle name, but if anyone outside of my family calls me this, I don't respond. Well, sometimes I do, but it's not pretty.)

As I got older, the letters got longer. Though she had little formal education, Myrna knew how to apply her intelligence and had learned foreign languages. She'd write me in Arabic or French and include a vocabulary translation in the back. She encouraged me to read and learn as much as I could.

Myrna's visits were like royalty coming to town. She wore African clothes and looked regal. A talented painter and photographer, she sometimes used me as a subject. I always sat very still and she'd say I was a perfect model. It made me proud to be the perfect anything.

Myrna's voice was like a flowing river, calm and filled with musical inflections. In my mother's house, even when we were calm, we'd be screaming and yelling, talking at the same time. Myrna would always wait until things had almost calmed down to add her comments.

Myrna called me Bess-One, her number one. She'd tell me African folk tales and would let me help her paint. I used to think that our backyard on Gordon Street was full of trees, but there was only one tree. All the others I remember came from Myrna's paintings.

Myrna would tell me that God loved me and that no matter how alone I was, God was with me. She would share things with me as if we were the same age. Sometimes I wished she hadn't. She had lots of boyfriends and one was married. She told me that this man had gotten her pregnant and she had miscarried in the toilet. I didn't fully understand what she was talking about. "I'm just twelve," I told her. And we cried together.

In 1967, Myrna asked my mother if I could come to visit her in New York. She told my mother that it was just for the summer, but we secretly hoped it would last forever. New York was bigger than she had described it. I was frightened by the crowded sidewalks and loud noises. She took me everywhere we went. Her friends all remarked on how similar we looked and wondered if I were really her daughter. I secretly wished Myrna was my mother. I would slur the name Myrna so that it sounded like "Mommy." She never corrected me.

Myrna had a beautiful boyfriend who was also an artist. He was Muslim. He treated me like someone special. He tested my abilities with mind benders and trick problems. *A man is found hanging by his neck in a room that's locked from the inside. There's no furniture, but there's a puddle of water under him. Was it murder or suicide? And how did it happen?* Days would go by, but he never gave me the answer. I had to figure it out just like you do.

No man had ever spent so much time with me or had given me so much attention. I wanted to stay in New York forever. Here I had a family closer to what I saw on TV. A few more kids and we could buy a school bus and start a band.

One day, when Myrna and I were on the subway, a little girl about my age whispered in my ear. She said that if I drank milk, the rats would come out of the sewers at night and suck my tongue. I was horrified. After that I refused to drink milk or eat anything that had milk in it. I was so frightened that I couldn't sleep.

Myrna thought I was homesick. I wasn't. I didn't want to go back with those crazy people, but I didn't want the rats to suck my tongue either. I didn't tell Myrna the rat story, but I cried all the time. She took me back to Wilmington.

Myrna's sense of responsibility toward our family didn't end there. Eventually she moved back in with us to try to help us out, but her anger toward my mother for giving her up, combined with my mother's conviction that Myrna thought she was better than the rest of us, made the house like a powder keg. (All right, an even bigger powder keg.) So Myrna left. She traded her mother's crazy house for her father's, moving in to care for him as his health declined. She gave up her painting, her study of language, and replaced them with alcohol.

Learning the Hard Way

Myrna had been drawn back to Wilmington to fill a void left in our house when Chris moved out. Chris had been the backbone of our family. She not only fed, cleaned, and disciplined us, she gave us a sense of who we were. She didn't feel like my sister until I got older. As a child I thought she was my second mother. She was.

Chris always told us, "Berry may not mean a lot right now, but someday it will." She said that people would someday honor the name Berry and proclaim, "Do tell, you're one of the Delaware Berrys. How mahvelous."

Chris is funny and smart, resourceful and inquisitive, but others would call her tough. Her greatest talent is keeping things in perspective. She calls things as she sees them. While others try to be diplomatic, Chris always says the first thing that comes to mind. I knew from an early age that she was fearless because she did the impossible: She argued and fought with our mother.

She tells me now that, while growing up, she was constantly afraid—afraid that she'd accidently do something wrong and harm us, afraid that my mother would one day leave her with us, afraid that she'd never have a life of her own. When she thought we weren't looking, she'd silently cry. Huge tears would stream down her beautiful face. I wanted to comfort her but I was afraid to. Afraid that whatever could make *her* cry might still be hanging around.

But Chris had a way of making us feel that everything would

be okay even if she didn't believe it herself. Whenever my mother was late with payments and bill collectors would come around, Chris would turn out the lights and have us sit quietly until they left. Sometimes, though, she'd open the door wide and scream into the face of those bill collectors. "Do you think you're going to get blood out of a turnip, mister?" she'd yell. "If so, come and show me how, please show me how."

You never knew how Chris would respond to something. Her punishments hardly ever matched the crime.

Wilmington was like other cities in the sixties—it had its share of racial unrest. (Has anything racial ever been restful?) Sometimes people would throw rotten eggs at our house. We suspected the Dineens, a White family whose backyard was on the opposite side of the garages. Chris says now that she always felt bad about those eggs. She felt that people were trying to tell us that *we* were rotten, too.

After one such egg assault, I decided to be as bold as my big sister Chris. I marched around to the Dineenses' house and found Janet, the youngest child, who was also my playmate. I didn't see any eggs around, but that didn't matter.

"You're nothing but a no-good, dirty White cracker," I said to her.

My mother would curse like a sailor, but we were never allowed to curse or use racial slurs. There was something about the way the word *cracker* rolled off my tongue and the way it made Janet look that gave me a sense of power. Something in my mind must have snapped because I kept going.

"And your mama's a cracker, your daddy's a cracker, even your old, dirty dog, Jerry, is a cracker. Cracker dog, cracker dog . . . the cracker's got a cracker dog."

Janet was in tears. She ran into her house and told her mother. Who called my aunt Gladys. Who called Chris.

Within minutes, Chris was standing in the doorway yelling, "Bessie, get your Black ass in this house." I marched home fantasizing about how Chris would take my side. How she, too, understood the evil of White crackers and would secretly help me end their bedevilment.

When I got to the house, Chris was standing in the doorway. I was smiling at first, but something in her eyes told me to wipe the silly grin off my face. I ducked under Chris's arm and she calmly sent me to the kitchen. She was so calm that I was frightened.

She told me to go to the cupboard and get the box of crackers. I did and she told me to look at it.

Then the dam broke.

"Does this look like Janet?" she roared.

"N-n-n-n-no," I stammered.

"Then why the hell did you call her that?"

Without waiting for a reply, Chris beat me with the box of crackers. Once the box was crumpled and the crackers were scattered all over the floor, she found a belt and kept beating me. I got a lot of beatings, but this was the worst. I probably don't need to tell you that I can't look at a saltine without flinching.

While I was cleaning up my mess, as Chris called it, she explained to me why she snapped. She said that I would see a lot of stupidity in my life, but just because others were stupid didn't give me an excuse to be stupid with them. I had to be proud and find better ways to deal with ignorance. "Name-calling and violence is not the way," she said. The look on her face said she knew she'd been guilty, too.

Much later, when I became a comedienne and was doing 250 appearances a year, I was constantly on the road. Every night was a different city and a different hotel. I saw more white sheets than David Duke. Every day someone in the hotel would mistake me for the maid. They'd ask me for towels or stop me in the hall to say they needed soap. At first I wanted to scream and call them all dirty melba toast—'cause I can't say cracker anymore. But Chris had planted the seed that taught me to find another way. Humor had become my way.

Once when I had just arrived at a hotel where I'd be doing stand-up that evening, a man walked up to me and said, "You can come in my room and do your job now."

I didn't scream or protest. I walked into his room and told some jokes.

As much as Chris understood about the world, she felt trapped by her responsibility of taking care of four kids. When the fifth one arrived, my sister Tanya, Chris had to get out. She slept with the first man who asked her and got pregnant. She was always a big woman, so over the next nine months, we just thought she was becoming a bigger woman. When she started screaming in pain, even my mother, the nurse's aide, didn't know what was going on. Finally we rushed her to the hospital.

She came home with a son, Christopher Alan Berry, but soon she was gone. It was just around the corner to another house, but it felt like a world away.

Baby in Our Family

My sister Tanya, the straw that broke Chris's back, was a surprise to the rest of us kids, let alone to my mother, who was forty-nine. I was six.

Tanya has had her share of issues to deal with, but she has managed to stay out of many of the family's cycles. Maybe this is because we were always so relentless in telling her that she wasn't really a part of the family.

Tanya had the lightest skin, dark, almond-shaped eyes, a tiny nose, and ruby lips. She was the most beautiful baby I had ever seen. Because my mother and Chris had to work, Tanya lived for the first five years of her life with my aunt Catherine and my uncle Bus, who spoiled her rotten. By the time Tanya came to live with us, she was used to getting her way. My mother felt guilty about not raising her, so she'd always take her side.

Since our mother would never punish her, we kids took up the slack. We told her that she'd been found in the snow, which was why her skin was so much lighter than ours. We called her the Snow Queen, but when my mother was around, we'd call her Princess. My mother thought this was a term of endearment and started to call Tanya Princess, too. Finally Tanya blabbed and we got our butts beat.

Tanya was determined to keep showing us how different she was. She was bright enough to learn to read early, and she read every word she saw. A bus trip with her was like being with Vanna White on speed: "Stop. S-T-O-P. Stop. Oooh, I know what that spells. Retail. R-E-T-A-I-L. Retail. Liquor Store. L-I-Q-U-O-R . . ."

We would try to cover her mouth, but Tanya would run like the wind. Even then she could escape when the rest of us couldn't.

It's Not My Fault . . .

If not having a father around and not knowing who he was became an issue for me in adulthood, it was harder on my two brothers much earlier. Brent and Kevin had similar reactions to the situation, but they took very different forms.

Brent is six years older than I am. During our childhood, he was the toughest Berry that ever lived. He was small for his age, but what he lacked in size he made up for with guts and fierce determination. He was hell-bent on showing the world what he could do.

Kids would tease Brent about not having a father, about his Goodwill clothes and run-over shoes. So he'd get into fights to shut them up. Since he was the oldest boy, he felt he had to protect all of us.

Once, when a gang of White boys had been terrorizing our neighborhood with racial slurs and random attacks, Brent and his buddies found these boys and gave them the beating of their lives. To retaliate, they waited to get Brent when he was alone. They climbed on top of the garages across the street from our house. When Brent came home they threw rocks, broken bottles, and scrap metal at him.

Luckily, his screams brought us and some neighbors to his rescue. The injuries were severe enough to require twenty stitches to his head. He vowed to kill them all. We knew he'd make good on his threat, so my mother didn't let him go anywhere but school.

One night my mother sent me to the store. It was getting dark so she told me to go quickly; after Brent's attack we had to be careful, On my way back from the store, a group of young Black boys jumped out from the side of a building and grabbed me. One yelled, "Take her bag." Another said, "Get her money." The biggest boy stood in front of me and said, "I'm going to make her 'do it.'"

Then one of the gang recognized me and said, "Man, that's *Berry's* sister." I knew that they meant Brent. At that moment I saw fear on *their* faces.

They handed my bag back to me and tried to act real nice. "Please don't tell Berry about this," they pleaded. "Yeah, don't tell him," someone else echoed. Then he gave me a dime. I don't know what Brent had done to them or what they had seen him do, but he struck fear in their hearts. He struck fear in mine, too.

When teachers would complain to my mother about Brent's fighting, he'd say it wasn't his fault. Sometimes it wasn't, but sometimes it was. Brent developed the habit of shifting responsibility off on other people.

He broke into the King Center on Market Street just around the corner from our house. Brent was very good at climbing and was very limber. According to him, some bigger boys *made* him climb to the second-story window of the center and then come down and let them in. They broke into the soda machine and stole a few bottles and the change. Strictly small potatoes—but they got caught.

This was at a time when people knew what was going on in their neighborhoods and they didn't mind getting involved. Somebody called the police and somebody else called the boys' parents.

My mother told the police to lock my brother up and throw away the key. She said that she'd never have a thief for a son. The police put Brent through the entire routine, making him believe he was being arrested. When he got home, my mother beat him mercilessly.

Brent never tried to steal anything again.

He was the darkest of the kids. Among Blacks, dark skin is not usually thought of as beautiful and is very often considered negative. We were cruel to Brent about his color, and because he had been labeled a thief, he got the nickname Black Bart. He hated this.

Brent was also radical before it was hip. He'd say things like, "I go to school because the Man don't want to see me educated." Chris would correct him, "No, fool, you go to school because Mom would kick your Black ass if you didn't."

That was the way Brent operated. Nothing was ever his fault, but he needed to feel he was in control. If anything was pushed on him, if anybody said, "You must do this," he'd either rebel and have nothing to do with it or come up with a way to be sure we knew he was doing things on his own terms.

But Kevin felt responsible for everything.

. . . *It's All My Fault*

Kevin was truly my best pal while we were growing up. He can still make me laugh with a look. He is absolutely driven by a need to know how things work and how he can make them work better. When we were kids, nothing was safe: telephones, radios, TVs. My mother would beat him for it, but he'd do it anyway.

After a while Kevin started punishing himself. Whenever he did something that he knew he shouldn't have, he'd sit himself down in the corner with his face to the wall. He wouldn't speak, not even to say what he'd done.

But Kevin wasn't just curious; he had a knack for finding a practical application for almost anything he encountered. He'd help people fix cars in the green garages, and often they'd pay him in spare parts. Kevin would use these parts to build homemade bikes and go-carts. He called them "rides." I loved it when he took me for a spin. We'd go racing down Gordon Street screaming at the top of our lungs.

One man that Kevin helped with his car owned a bright yellow guitar. Kevin saw it and was determined to have it. He struck a deal with the guy—he offered to work for a month in exchange for that guitar. He couldn't play the guitar or any other instrument, but he wanted to learn. When he finally earned that guitar, he carried it across the street like he was the Black Gene Autry. He was strumming and picking and making all kinds of noises. We told him that he was stupid and that instead of the guitar he should have taken money. But Kevin had resolved to learn to play the guitar. He was nine and he did exactly what he said.

Soon Kevin was really playing and he would sing songs that he made up. Sometimes, when my mother was in a good mood, we'd sit around and sing songs together. We'd all take turns performing and cracking each other up. My mother would sing her own brand of the blues:

> *Lord, I got all these nappy-headed children*
> *and they won't listen to me.*
> *I got seven children, I should have stopped at three*

Kevin seemed to have a need to bring joy and laughter into our house. He was excellent at memorizing and could recite whole passages from scripture, but what he liked best were lines from movies. He'd take on the role of characters from *Sounder* and practically recite the entire script. When I finally got to see my first James Bond movie—which was nowhere near as good as Kevin's descriptions—I was shocked to learn that the cast was not Black.

"What made you think they were Black?" Kevin asked.

"'Cause you told it like they were," I replied.

Kevin's sense of responsibility has stayed with him his whole life. He's made a career out of the Marines, where he is an expert marksman and an instructor. When he comes to visit me, he's barely out of his gleaming, customized car—"Berry's ride" they call it on base—before he's fixing the wiring in the house, clearing out the brush in some overgrown part of the yard so far away I don't even know I own it, and taking time with all the kids. The kids adore him and they respect him. Kevin functions as a father, filling a role for them that no one was around to fill for him.

How my brothers interacted with me, and with other women, had a great impact on my own expectations about relationships with men. I'd hear them talk about women in a crude way, and I knew that if my own brothers who loved me treated women like that, then strangers would treat me that way also. After they were married, I watched their relationships with their wives. Because they had seen my mother work hard, they vowed to take care of their wives completely. This didn't always work, but they tried. "My wife will never need a job," they proclaimed. I hated their attitudes. "I will always work," I'd tell them. "Good, because nobody will want to marry you anyway," they'd say.

Their idea of marriage was based on the fact that they were men who hadn't seen the relationship between husbands and wives. My idea of marriage was derived from the fact that I was a woman who hadn't seen the relationship between husbands and wives. They had seen a woman work as hard as she could to support a family and decided that it was their job to prevent it from happening in their home. It was almost like they were trying to make up for all those times when they wanted to help our mother and couldn't.

I had seen a woman work as hard as she could and learned that I could always rely on myself.

The Pretty One

If Tanya had that little extra bit of determination that it took to break free of many of my mother's cycles, our sister Portia did not. Portia is four years older than me, and she was always the pretty one. When we were very young, Portia wore a pair of those cat-shaped eyeglasses, powder blue with rhinestones. We nicknamed her Cateyes.

Portia was the only one of my siblings whose father ever visited. Emerson would come loaded with presents. He'd always bring along his wife and their daughter. He would go on and on about how cute his baby Portia was.

"Isn't she cute?" he asked us, as if we were going to hold up scorecards: *9.1, 9.4, 8.9, 9.5.*

Even though I felt excluded, I loved Emerson and his wife for caring about my sister. They'd even spend their holidays with us. This is not uncommon among people of color when children are involved. They often ignore old disagreements and lost loves as everyone becomes family with the same unspoken goal: to do what's best for the children.

Portia would spend the summers with her father; my mother wouldn't allow her to stay any longer. She would come back with new clothes and all the latest records and toys. She'd hold them up and dare us to touch her new things. I did. When she wasn't looking, I'd take her new dolls and punch their heads in.

Portia was always talented and dramatic. Chris used to call her "the Gloria Swanson of the Ghetto." If Portia fell down and scraped her knee, she acted as if she were dying. I knew she was acting, because she was tough. Portia could fight like Jack Johnson. I once saw her stuff a girl in a locker.

By the time she reached high school, Portia was the most popular, most beautiful, most everything girl there. She was head cheerleader, drum majorette, and president of the dance troupe. She was "Miss It." I not only wanted to be like her, I wanted to be her.

When Portia wasn't around and I wasn't performing plastic surgery on her dolls, I'd put on her clothes and try to act like her. I was a Portia-vestite. I'd race to put things back just as she left them, but there was always one sleeve a little out of place. She would notice and beat me up.

One time I wore her slip. It was hanging below my dress and one of Portia's girlfriends said, "It's snowing down south." Portia realized, almost without looking, that it was her slip. She attacked me and made me take it off in front of her girl-friends.

"Get your big ol' butt out of my slip. Look at her big butt, y'all."

When people found out I was Portia's sister, they couldn't believe it. They'd say things like, "Really? You mean her blood sister?" They acted as if I were some alien trying to associate myself with the best human on the planet. But I proclaimed my relationship because I was proud. Portia was somebody.

The Cycle Continues

But all Portia's sense of style and beauty didn't keep her from being my mother's daughter. My mom warned us all about making the mistakes she had made. "You're going to end up with a house full of babies and nobody to help you."

Portia didn't listen. She went looking for love just as Mom had and found it on a two-way street—Gordon Street. At the bottom of Gordon Street, to be exact, in the Thunderguards' clubhouse. At this point, Portia already had a child, and I'm sure she was just trying to find her a daddy like my mother had done.

Portia's love was one of the head guys in the club. Now I

don't think everybody in a motorcycle gang is bad. Some of my best friends are in motorcycle gangs. Okay, they're not, but I know some. You can imagine our dismay when Portia told us she was moving in with this man. The relationship may have been beautiful at some point, but I didn't see it. It soon became abusive.

My siblings and I were often called to the rescue. It's funny how closely a family can huddle in times of trouble. No matter how strained the family relationship, when trouble breaks out, everyone comes running to help.

Portia told us she'd been threatened, whipped, hit with a TV set, and God only knows what else before she finally left her Thunderguard. But by the time she did, she had another child.

Nori, Portia's first child, was born loving her mother. If Portia went out, which she often did, Nori would cry all night until she returned. She'd cling to her mother and declare, "My mommy is the best mom in the whole world."

"Yeah, right," Chris would say, while thinking the exact opposite. Portia did shower Nori with all the love she could muster, but she spent most of her time somewhere else. In her way, she was trying to make a better life for herself and Nori by trying to find a man who could love them both. This was an old pattern in our family.

Portia's son William was just a baby when Portia moved out of that Thunderguard's house. William had bright eyes and was beautiful. However, he had seen things that children should never witness, terrible things. These things are not for me to tell. They're a part of William's story.

Portia tried to keep her family together—by finding another man. This is hard for me to understand. Portia had more talent and opportunities than any of my other brothers and sisters; she could look at our mother's life and see what didn't work. She carried the scars of an abusive relationship. Still she went looking for another man. She found him and had another child, Jabril.

Nori became the primary caregiver for her two young siblings, living out the same cycles that Chris had experienced. At this point I longed to take care of her, but I couldn't. I was in graduate school and performing all over the country.

Portia moved to Dover, Delaware—my mother's hometown—still caught in those cycles. But unlike my mother, she didn't become an alcoholic; she became a crack addict, just three miles from the plantation where my great-grandmother had lived. This is entirely too close to be a coincidence. Unable to provide for her children, she was on welfare and moving from place to place. She was pregnant with her fourth child when she moved in with Myrna, who was also living in Dover.

After years of caring for her sick father, Myrna had become distressed by life's problems, giving up her painting, and like my mother, had become an alcoholic. This was dangerous because she was severely diabetic. But when Portia moved in, Myrna had taken up painting once more, was in recovery, and had been dry for about two years. There was hope for both of them until Myrna started drinking again. She called me every night to ask me for guidance. We'd talk and I'd send money to help ease the burden and to help Portia get out on her own. I asked Myrna never to tell Portia where the money came from. A year before, I had told Portia that until she changed her life, I wouldn't send any more money. I didn't want her to think that the bank had reopened.

Myrna helped Portia move across the street. Myrna was putting her life back in order, but the stress, drinking, and diabetes were all too much. My beautiful sister Myrna died.

I had just finished the pilot for *The Bertice Berry Show* and was back on the road doing stand-up. I was tired of all the family pressures and decided not to check my messages for three days. When I finally did, I learned that Myrna had died and that my family had been trying to reach me. I was alone in a hotel room in Vermont and I cried all night.

The next day a student from the college where I had performed took me to the airport. I told her about Myrna and she became sad. By then I was okay. Myrna had spoken to me and let me know that I had another angel and I could talk to her anytime I wanted. Like long distance—only free.

I had other engagements, but I decided to go home only because my mother needed me. The news of my sister's death, and her unresolved differences with Myrna, sent my mother back to the bottle. If it hadn't been for this, I would have completed the last two days of my tour and gone home for the funeral.

On the way to the airport, I noticed a sign for an authentic African import shop. In Vermont? I asked the student to take me there. She agreed and we were soon lost in the woods. Eventually we found the place and it was a treasure. The shop was in a house that was owned by a woman who could tell you not only where everything had come from but also the name of the person who had made it. I found a dress that reminded me of Myrna and the time I had lived with her in New York.

When I got to Delaware, the funeral director told me that almost all the arrangements had been handled by Gwen, Myrna's cousin. The only chore left was finding something for Myrna to wear; did I have any suggestions? I told him I could do better and I produced the African dress from the shop in Vermont. It was perfect.

Burying Myrna was hard on us all, especially my mother.

I've always heard about how painful it is for a parent to bury a child; I saw that pain in my mother's face.

As I was about to leave, Chris told me that she couldn't handle the stress of our family any longer. She said that she'd been taking care of us all of her life and that she wanted a life of her own. Without a moment's hesitation, I told her to come and live with me and that I would take care of her until she could sort things out for herself. She said thank you and let's go. We did.

I don't know what made me make this offer. I was about to start *The Bertice Berry Show,* which meant I would finally be living and working in the same city. I was just divorced and I was thinking about the possibility of finding a good relationship and starting my own family. But God works in mysterious ways.

Chris and I adjusted easily and were getting into a comfortable rhythm when we got word from my mother that tragedy had struck again.

Portia's cocaine addiction had gotten worse and her children were in danger of being taken away. The child protective services counselor wanted to know if any family member could take them; if not, they were in danger of being split up.

Chris and I cried for about five minutes. We cried for Portia and her children, and we cried for ourselves and the loss of our newfound freedom. We called our mother back and told her that we'd be there to get the children.

Now, none of this was like any of the dreams that I had created for myself. It hit at a moment when it seemed like all my carefully laid plans were bearing fruit and my career was going to take a big leap forward. And I knew—at least in an abstract way that didn't involve thoughts of diaper changing, lost bus passes, and homework assignments—that kids would change many things.

The timing of my mother's call was amazing. Different syndication companies were bidding for me as their next talk-show host. Huge sums of money were in play and rising quickly. The signing deal that was worth $100,000 one day was worth $500,000 the next. Fox had been very interested in me, but their bid was only about half what the other companies offered. Money was important, but it wasn't the most important thing. I wanted to have some say in what I was doing. Fox promised more creative control, so it was worth it to me to listen when they wanted to talk some more.

They took me out to dinner in Los Angeles to some restaurant with a name I couldn't pronounce. I was the only Black woman in the restaurant, sitting at a table surrounded by powerful White men. Not the mid-level people who do all the work but the big boys who make all the decisions: Greg Meidel, president of 20th Century–Fox's television division, and Kenny Solomon, head of sales. They were making their pitch, doubling their offer, going on about percentages and overhead amortization.

In the middle of dinner I dropped my bomb. "I'm going to be a mother."

The table went silent. I could hear what was rushing into their heads: Shit, we just spent all this money trying to win this woman over and she's going to be a single mother. Who does she think she is? Murphy Brown?

I smiled a big smile and waited for somebody to choke out a congratulations.

"Er, um, how soon?" somebody gasped.

"Next week. Triplets."

Somebody get the smelling salts.

I eventually explained what was going on, and they looked as relieved as if I'd just told them I'd work for free. Kenny

Solomon's wife was pregnant and due soon, and we talked about how we thought parenthood would change our lives. Either Kenny was holding something back or we both got a long series of rude shocks a few weeks later.

When Chris and I arrived in Delaware, the situation was worse than I expected. Portia and the children were living in filthy conditions. We'd been poor but we were never dirty. Portia had always been very clean, but crack destroys all reason. The child-services counselor told us that this wasn't the worst case they'd seen, but the children deserved better.

By now Portia had given birth to another daughter, Fatima, who was only four months old. Nori was living with her godmother, but we were also giving a home to William, who was eight, and Jabril, who was only a year and a half old. All of them had special needs. When it came to children, I didn't have a clue, and Chris's son was in his twenties and she could barely remember it. But we had more resources than my mother ever had and we put them to use.

Portia gave us a hard time but thanked us profusely. She knew that giving up the children was the right thing to do. I had never seen her like this and I was ashamed. But I was more pissed than embarrassed. How could she put her children through something like this? Especially when her own childhood had been so hard. She performed a piece from *Who's Afraid of Virginia Woolf?*—she was cursing one minute and crying the next. Then she promised us that she'd get better and that she'd be coming for the kids soon.

Chris and I got all of the necessary paperwork taken care of, and we packed the children into the car for the thirteen-hour ride home to Chicago. We thought that they would cry for their mother, but they didn't. When we loaded the youngest two into the car first, William thought he was being left behind. He looked at us tearfully and begged, "Please don't leave me. Take me, too." We explained that he'd never be left again. We packed him in and took off.

I didn't know the correct way to attach a baby's car seat. The infant should face the seat, but I had it turned the other way. Fatima rode across country slumped over. I thought there was something wrong with her motor skills, and every five minutes I reached around to push her up straight. Thank God children are resilient.

We stopped in Wilmington to purchase some of the things our wild and crazy bachelorette life in Chicago hadn't included: high chairs, baby swings, playpens. The children had nothing and we worked to fit everything we could into that car.

Sometimes your life path takes one of its bends and you have to roll with it. I was on the road to success when the children came, and then I had to change paths. Both paths can get me to success; they just do it from different directions.

CHAPTER THREE

Fatherhood Found

When I was a kid, other kids made fun of me because I didn't have a father.

"You don't have a father. You don't have a father."

I'd go running home, hyperventilating the way kids do when they cry. Luckily, my mother went to the Moms Mabley school for rearing children. She'd give me advice from one of Moms Mabley's routines:

"Oh, stop crying. You tell those children not to talk about the dead unless it's good. Your father's dead. Good."

*T*alk-show guests often blame others for their troubles. They've moved from the "Why me?" syndrome of the seventies and eighties to the "I'm-like-this-because-of-my-parents" syndrome of the nineties. They're all good at finding fault with everyone but themselves.

We heard so much blaming during the taping of *The Bertice Berry Show* that Sol Feldman, our producer, came up with the idea of a show called "Families Who Can't Function Without Dysfunction."

It was one big "Mommy-made-me-do-it" fest. The day's expert was Patti Davis, daughter of Ronald and Nancy Reagan. She was brilliant. She pointed out that while many of her problems stemmed directly from a dysfunctional relationship with her family, she had decided to move on with her life.

We talked about our childhoods. I told her that I had forgiven my mother long before she'd asked for forgiveness. Patti was astonished by this and told me that this was a sign that I had been here before. Whatever, I thought. I had too many problems of my own to be lugging my mother's around.

As a sociologist, I understand that our parents have a tremendous influence on our worldview—good and bad. Many people find comfort in wallowing in old hurts and misunderstandings. I'm always looking for a way to put them behind me.

Feel the Hurt but Let It Go

When my mother gave me that piece of advice (feel the hurt but let it go), I thought it was because she was the primary source of most of my pain and was looking for a way to avoid the blame. Then I realized that she had had more hurts and disappointments than any ten ordinary people could have endured. She had learned that to survive she couldn't relive the same pains over and over again.

Sometimes her pain did become mine and her burdens became my burdens. Getting rid of them was not as easy as taking them on. Yet it was something that I had to do. I know her relationships with men have had an impact on my relationships with men, but not because I patterned my life after hers; quite the contrary.

It was because I didn't know my father.

I didn't know who my father was until I was thirty years old. This was something that, for the most part, hadn't really bothered me. Oh, sure, I used to dream that some wealthy man might show up someday and say, "Yes, Bertice, I am here to take you away." But many children have this dream. Don't they?

I had always assumed that, with the exception of Portia, my brothers and sisters and I had the same father. This man, we were told, had died.

But something in my spirit told me otherwise. My mother says I would repeatedly ask where my real father was. She told me that as a young girl I always wanted to know. That I even once told her that I needed to know because one day I'd be famous and didn't want some stranger saying he was my father. I don't remember my doing this, but my mother does.

In fact, I don't remember asking about my father until college. I was in my dorm room listening to Chuck Mangione's *Children of Sanchez* album. A short song on it talked about a Daddy saying good-bye and about how the child had already missed him. The child said that she loved her mother very much, but the mother could not replace the father.

I played that song over and over again. And I wept for the father I had missed. I called my mother and asked about my father. I wanted details, a picture, or anything that she could give me.

My mother can be very stubborn. She changed the subject as if I had never asked. Now you may think of her as cruel, yet she felt that this information was her business, and her business only.

Her business. The phrase still echoes in my head.

My mother didn't discuss the men in her life with her children. As far as I know, she probably never talked about them with anybody. The closest she came was getting drunk with Aunt Gladys and crying over Al Green songs.

"Love and Happiness" was one of her favorites. Whenever the song got to the part that said "Love will make you do wrong," they'd start testifying. "Yes, yes, yes. Talk about it, Al. Yes, it will," they'd cry. My cousins and I would laugh. It was only when I was older that I began to understand what she was crying about.

Be Careful What You Ask For

At age thirty, nearly a decade after that phone call to my mother inspired by Chuck Mangione, I read a book about mother-daughter relationships. The book wasn't that great—if it were, I'd tell you the name—but it made me think of my mother, so I decided to call her and thank her for all she'd done for me. I realized that whatever trouble and strife my mother had brought to my existence, I was still here and I was doing okay.

That day had been particularly difficult for my mom. A friend of hers had died and Mom was the one who had found the body. She was sad for the loss of yet another friend and feeling, at seventy-three, that her time might be coming soon.

"I want to tell you about your father," she said.

"Okay," I replied calmly, having no idea what was coming next. All I knew was that this had been a taboo subject and now all of a sudden she was bringing it up. "Why are you telling me this now? You've always said that it was your business."

"Well, now it's yours."

At first she played her all-too-familiar guessing game. This was a contest she started whenever she knew she had information you desperately wanted. My mom had me where she wanted me, and if I wanted to know more, I'd have to play the game.

"Now, who are you named after?" she asked.

"Bertice Redding, the singer." I had learned through bits and pieces of information that my mother had named me after a Black singer/actress who, like Josephine Baker, Bricktop, and Nina Simone, had met far greater success in Europe than here in the good old U.S. of A.

"And what's her last name?" Mom could play this game out indefinitely.

"Come on, Mom, I've already said Redding." I was getting tired of this game quicker than usual.

"And that's who your father is," she said triumphantly.

84

"Okay, Mom, please tell me how Bertice Redding can be my father," I demanded, getting a little more testy than any daughter should.

Then she said it. "Not Bertice Redding. Otis Redding."

I paused for a second and thought that maybe my mother had fallen off the wagon or something. Or that maybe the death of her friend had been more than she could handle and she was finally going off the deep end.

I quickly got back in the game. "You mean Otis 'Sitting on the Dock of the Bay' Redding?"

"That's the one."

"Right, so who's my brothers' father? Bill Cosby or Stevie Wonder?"

My mother went dead silent and held that silence long enough for me to remember the concept of respect. I apologized for being fresh, as she called it, and tried to take this seriously.

I flipped through my mind and quickly remembered that Otis Redding had died in a plane crash when I was around seven. This meant, of course, that I'd have no chance of meeting him here on earth, and I was right back where I'd started, fatherless. I also remembered that he was quite young when he died and that my mother was already middle-aged when I was born. That meant nothing in the scheme of things, I realized, since she has always looked at least twenty-five years younger than her age.

(My mother has flawless skin, is quick-witted, and has a smile that won't quit and charm to match. My older sisters have told me that she has always turned heads. She could attract any man, be he Black or White, rich or poor, old or young. She's always been a torch.)

I asked my mother all kinds of questions about how she'd

met Otis Redding: how many times she'd seen him, what he was like, if he had known about me . . . and if she was sure.

My mother said she'd known him from the "Big Time" performance nights in Chester, Pennsylvania. He was playing there when they met, and from what I gathered, they'd had a one-night stand. She never saw him or even tried to contact him after that. She said of course she was sure, but she had always felt that no one would believe her if she said so, and she wondered why they should. I wanted to know why she hadn't at least told me before.

She paused for some time and then started crying.

"I didn't want this to hurt any more than it already has."

Mom said she didn't want me to go searching for a dead father and stirring things up that didn't need to be bothered. She'd known that he had a wife and children, and this had embarrassed her greatly. We cried together, and it was then that she asked for my forgiveness.

"For what?" I asked. "For giving me life?"

We hung up.

Congratulations, Sort Of

Up till this point, when people asked me about my father, a normal question, I'd tell them he was dead.

"I'm sorry," they'd always say.

"Why, did you kill him?" I'd ask.

No one ever knew quite how to take this cavalier attitude about my father's death. Then when I explained that I never knew him and therefore hadn't really missed him, they tried to sympathize. But this new information about my father's identity changed everything.

I tried to discuss my feelings with some of my closest friends. They congratulated me as if I'd won something. This angered me. I'd worked hard all my life and nothing I'd done had ever been received with so much praise and attention. It was like finishing first in a marathon but only getting your picture in the paper because you ran into John Kennedy Jr. on the way.

I wanted to know more but didn't know yet what I wanted to do with this new information. Chris and my business manager, Terry, both suggested I hire a private investigator. I hadn't yet been offered any TV deals, but I felt they'd be coming soon. I didn't want anybody finding out about this in some weird way that would affect my chance of realizing my dreams, so I opted to just keep it quiet.

With the help of my publicist, David Brokaw, I hired one of the best private investigators in the business. He contacted my mother and pried even further into her life, which embarrassed her even more. "In my day, people didn't air their dirty laundry," she said.

The private investigator determined that what my mother had told him couldn't be disproved, but without biological tests or documents, it couldn't be proved either.

Well, thanks, I thought. I'm no closer to the facts than I was before. Terry informed me that I was closer: I had my mother's word and a picture of Otis Redding.

I didn't know what to do next. I decided not to contact his family for the same reasons my mother never had. I was in the throes of a divorce, and, God knows, I couldn't stand another rejection. So I held on to it. I didn't want the Redding family thinking that I wanted something from them, 'cause I had made my own way in life. I didn't need their help and I certainly didn't want their name. I've always liked the sound of my own name: It is musical and it is mine.

After I got the talk show and had heard hundreds of stories about folks looking for their families, I thought more about my own. I had to do something. It had been almost two years since I'd found out who my father was, but my life had been too filled by "more important things" to really focus on this revelation.

I'd found out where the Redding family lived, so one day out of nowhere I contacted one of Otis's sons. We ended up talking for some time, and I told him my whole life story. He was shocked. He was familiar with me from the talk show and was a fan, and so fortunately he didn't take me for a complete loon. He came to Chicago and we talked some more. Oddly enough, one thing we didn't talk about was Otis. We sort of picked up in the middle of a conversation like old friends. He told me his family had heard the news but that they didn't look very kindly on it, didn't even believe it was true.

I was mad that somebody would suggest that my mother was not truthful. To her I was already more special than she felt she deserved, and she was proud. She didn't need to make something up to make me more glamorous. And I certainly wasn't looking for any attention that might accompany the news that I was Otis Redding's daughter. When I'd told the Fox executives about my mother and Otis for fear that the information would get out in a way that would be painful to my mother, some of them had wanted me to use the information for publicity. They argued that as an unknown this would be just what I needed to launch my career. But I didn't want to be thought of as the daughter of anyone other than Beatrice or Christine Berry. They had raised me. Otis Redding might have provided me with some genes, but it's my mother's spirit that I had learned from, that had helped make me my own person. What I did with what she had given me was up to me.

All of the brouhaha over Otis Redding made me realize at least one thing: that no matter who my mother is and who my father was, I'm free to shape my own development. Yes, it is absolutely necessary to know and understand my mother's patterns of behavior and how they have influenced me. I was glad to know the identity of my father. But there is a fine line between trying to understand myself through my parents and using whatever I didn't have as an excuse. This is a line I am determined never to cross.

The Men in My Life

A large percentage of children in our society grow up without fathers. Some, like me, grow up having no idea who their father is. But just because a child doesn't have a responsible father nearby doesn't mean that there can't be a responsible male in the picture. Better yet, many responsible males. Now let me preach for a minute.

I'm sick and tired of hearing men run around and talk about how women are taking over. They feel that they should rule, that they should be in charge. Well, go for it. Tons of children are waiting for a man to say something positive to them. One act of kindness in the life of a fatherless child can make all the difference in the world. But too many men are unwilling to assume even this small role in children's lives.

I was fortunate to have had positive male role models in my life, men who became my surrogate fathers. One of these was my uncle Bus, who was married to my aunt Catherine (well, at least that's what we thought; they lived together and were in love); he was a character. The world's best cook, Uncle Bus talked to his food and it talked back.

"All right, li'l ol' crab. I'm going to put you in the boiling water. You're going to like it in here, crab."

We'd stand in the doorway listening, thinking he didn't know we were there. All of a sudden, he'd spin around with the crab in his hand and run after us.

"Save me. Save me. Save me."

I knew that crabs couldn't talk, but up until I started doing research for this book, I thought that crabs could scream. Uncle Bus was good.

Every year, Uncle Bus dressed up as Santa Claus and would come to our door with a small bag of gifts that meant the world to us. When he died, it seemed like all the laughter went with him. My aunt Catherine didn't seem the same without his sloppy kisses and talking foods. Nothing was.

My uncle Fred was Cousin Gladys's husband (yes, it's a Black thing and you *should* understand). He was a church-school janitor, but in my mind he was the principal. He'd bought an old school bus and would drive us all over the place. With his eight children and my mother's seven, people thought we were a choir, so he'd make us sing. We were probably awful, but to him we were destined to be the next Jackson 5. He was without a doubt the hardest-working man around.

As I got older, the fathers of my friends also went a long way to fill the void. My best friend Tia's father treated me as if I were his child. He praised me when I was good—and punished me when I wasn't. To this day, Mr. Thompson still doesn't hesitate to give me a talking-to, and to remind me that I'm never too grown-up for a butt-whipping.

Reverend Rainey, or Pop Pop, as we called the minister of my church, was my spiritual father. I've never met a man more committed to God's work. Never pompous or preachy, Pop

Pop was someone we all looked up to with great respect, but we weren't so much in awe of him that we didn't also feel very close to him. When I left for college, Pop Pop gave me two pieces of advice: to watch out for the boys and to acknowledge God in all things. He died two years ago, but sometimes I still hear his voice reminding me to acknowledge God in all things.

Ring Williams, my friend Rhonda's dad, single-handedly busts the negative stereotype of the Black man. He's hard-working, loyal, dedicated to his wife and family, and a fun-loving individual. Mr. Williams never sent his daughter a dime without sending the same amount to me. On the day I graduated from college without a single member of my family in the audience, it was Mr. Williams who escorted me from the platform after I received the President's Cup. His hand holding mine felt right.

Next came Terry Evenson, the rich father I had prayed for when I was a child. He came into my life at a time when he was most needed and helped to put me through college. Terry is a self-made millionaire who never brags or makes anyone feel uncomfortable. Whenever my friends meet Terry, they remark on how well he fits in as we discuss anything from the invasion of hip-hop to the invasion of Haiti. He's always been my friend and is now my business manager, having come into my professional life when I desperately needed his wisdom. We argue like other fathers and daughters must, but he tells me to do what I do best and he'll do what he does best, which, according to him, is everything. Whenever I am confronted with racial hatred or prejudice (sometimes my own), Terry reminds me of the big picture.

All of these men have had a positive impact on my life, so much so that when the subject of fatherless children comes up,

I think, how terrible, before I realize that the category includes me. But you know what, it doesn't have to be so terrible if each of the men who are around makes his contribution to the community.

Moving Forward

Each generation should be wiser than the last. That's what I believe is our responsibility, both in how we teach ourselves and how we raise our children. We must feel the pain that our ancestors have known, but we must let it go and move forward.

My generation of children was taught to revere and respect our parents. Now that we're parenting, we're told that we should think of our children as our friends. Confused by these seemingly opposite ideals, we achieve neither, unable to generate the closeness that we wish we could have had with our parents or to command the consideration and honor that it will take to raise our children right.

We can't blame our parents for not doing the things that we are only now learning ourselves. We must move onward and upward so that our children can blame us for all the things we haven't done right!

In raising my three kids, I'm still making some of the mistakes my mother made with me and my brothers and sisters, but not nearly as many and not nearly as often. In addition, I'm facing a lot of new problems, like how can I give them what I didn't have and still make sure they learn the same kind of responsibility and respect?

William, Jabril, and Fatima are teaching me how to receive love and how to give it unconditionally. They're teaching me patience and forcing me to be stable. When I was pushing myself to complete my education and then be a successful stand-up comic, I couldn't afford to focus on anything but that. The children are showing me that I need to expand my field of vision.

I often fast for spiritual insight or to cleanse my system. Fasting focuses me, centers me. I once got so busy fasting that I forgot the children hadn't eaten. Jabril climbed into a cabinet, got a bowl, and brought it to me.

"Cereal, please," he said with big, sad eyes. I was ashamed.

What was even funnier was when I realized that I actually had to clip the children's toenails. I made this discovery after hearing a strange tapping sound in my house, something like a large puppy running around. It took me a while to realize it was the kids—who knew?

But knowing these things gives me the power to change them.

I recently went home to visit my mother. I took her to her childhood home in Lebanon, Delaware. Chris and Tanya and the three kids went with us. Lebanon, Delaware, is about the size of a city block. The people who live there are still Black and still poor. My mother cried when she saw the place. Not much had changed in seventy years.

When we drove away, I realized how far my mother had come. But I was struck by a terrible revelation. We were only three miles from the crack house where Portia had lived with her children. With all the progress my mother has made, her children haven't gone quite far enough.

By claiming my mother's life and what I can know about my father, I have become free to discover all the forces that have shaped my family and, thus, me. Some are good: the desire to be free, the will to be educated, and the need to be spiritual. Some are negative: poverty, alcoholism, abuse, and fatherlessness. I'm really working on the last one; as a matter of fact, I'm taking applications.

CHAPTER FOUR

Relationship Rules

Today we're going to talk about male-female relationships. Don't worry, this is not going to be one of those "all men are dogs" sessions. They're not dogs, they're pigs.

But seriously, folks, men and women are extremely different. We've been taught to be. As a matter of fact, it's amazing that we get along at all. I'm constantly surprised that the majority of people in our society are heterosexual.

Please don't go tell your parents that Dr. Berry said that we should all become homosexual. What I'm saying is that we are socialized to interact better with people of our own gender. Then, by some miracle, we're supposed to go out and find someone of the opposite sex, marry them, and stay with them for the rest of our lives without ever being told how the other type thinks or lives.

A man and a woman will go on the same date and come back with completely different observations. The woman on the phone or in the dorm with her girlfriends:

"He's really cute, we like the same things, he's so polite. Did I tell you that he's a premed major? He's really cute. I think I've found him. This is Mr. Right."

Meantime the guy she went out with is somewhere telling his buddies, "What a body."

—from the lecture "Male-Female Relationships:
Can't Live with 'Em, Can't Shoot 'Em"

I should tell you that I've struggled with whether or not I should talk about relationships in this book. I kept thinking, Who am I to tell anybody else about 'em? I got a very late start dating, and my marriage that was going to last forever ended in divorce after only two years.

But then I realized that I've learned a great deal about relationships, precisely because I took the time to learn about myself and God first.

Besides, I was teaching human sexuality before I ever had sex, and no one walked away confused.

If You Can't Be with the One You Love, Love Yourself

Lately we've been bombarded with lectures and workshops dealing with the crisis of Black male-female relationships. I keep thinking, What crisis? Black people do and always will love each other. This so-called crisis is really an attempt to love one another better and a refusal to be loved any less than we deserve.

Against all odds and taking great risks, our enslaved ancestors did whatever they possibly could to be with their loved ones. And once slavery was abolished, the first thing the newly freed people did was to go looking for their families. Love and family are still at the center of our communities, of our very existence.

People talk about failed loves. How can love fail? Love conquers all. I've had several beautiful, nearly perfect relationships. When they ended, I still didn't define them as failures: They just weren't It. My friends tease me, saying that I go through men like I go through panty hose—and it's true that both are usually good for just one date. It's not that I'm being especially difficult or hard to please. It's just that I have standards.

Rule One

I have a rule that I always pay for the first three dates. If my date doesn't go for this, I don't go out with him again.

I don't want any man to think that I owe him or that he can buy me. Too often money becomes a means of control. By paying for the date myself, I'm not only eliminating that possibility, I'm also finding out early on if my independence will pose a problem. In any case, men shouldn't always have the burden of payment. There's nothing that says that because a man has a penis he also has to pay for dinner.

This is not a rule that I invented once I was successful and well known, a screening process to weed out gold diggers. But it is a rule that has everything to do with being the woman I have made myself into. As soon as I started to know and like myself, men started to like me, too. Now I have an abundance of choices and am making up for lost time.

Rule Two

Never go out on a first date alone. If the guy in question won't go out in a group, well, that's his loss. I still have a great evening planned with good friends.

You can learn a lot about a man by how he interacts in a group. Whether it's a group of his friends or mine, I can tell immediately how "real" he is. One-on-one, early in a relationship, men and women project false images of themselves: They want to impress, seduce.

I've had this rule for years, too, and it didn't start because I had a television show. If he cops an attitude, I tell him I'm a woman who likes herself and would like to get to know someone who's secure—and that *he's not it.*

Often I found myself dating men from other countries.

I loved their accents and their sensitivity. There's always something to learn when you're with someone from a place outside the United States. I'd bombard them with questions about their culture and how they perceived ours. Unfortunately, I only learned about their chauvinism later on . . . *un cochon est un cochon.* A pig is a pig.

My graduate school roommate, Bernita, would always tease me about what she still calls my "many suitors." She would reach for the ringing telephone and say, "Why am I answering it? I know it's for you.

"Burdize, te-le-phone," she'd say in a clipped accent.

"Who is it?"

"I don't know, but I know he's from Cameroon."

Once when one of these suitors called and asked me out, I told him it would be okay, but only if Bernita could come along.

He asked why, and I explained that we didn't really know each other well, and a third person would take some of the pressure off. He cursed me out in a language I didn't know and accused me of acting like his first wife.

"Oh, you're divorced?" I asked.

"No. She is still my first wife."

I don't remember everything about my response, but it had something to do with good riddance to bad garbage. It was too bad that he didn't understand me either.

Rule Three

Look for your soul mate. My mother says, "You could do bad by yourself."

I believe that I have a kindred spirit or soul mate out there, that this is the person with whom I can walk closely through this life. I believe that he's trying to get to me, but he's walking slowly . . . from a faraway place, a very faraway place.

I know that my spirit yearns to find the comfort that my great-grandmother Annie found in John Henry Freeman, to love someone fiercely and have that love reciprocated.

I've come close.

I met my first *boyfriend* in graduate school. He wasn't someone I just went out on a few dates with. This was a man about whom I thought, This could be it. To everyone's surprise, he was American.

We went to foreign films together and he cooked incredible meals for me. *I try not to stereotype, but this should have been my first clue:* He didn't try to grope me on our first date. *Clue number two.* He kissed me very lightly, flashed me his perfect smile, and then told me that he had enjoyed himself more than he'd expected (he hadn't expected to?) and wanted to go out again.

So we spent lots of time together. He left me notes and flowers and wrote letters to me even though we lived in the same small town. He was sweet and romantic. *Clue number three.*

But suddenly he stopped calling and didn't want to talk when I called him. *Clue number four.* Finally he said that he didn't want to see me anymore. I was heartbroken and needed an explanation. I suspected it was because I hadn't slept with him, and so I told him that if that was the problem we should do something about it. He assured me that that wasn't it, and even though I continued to plead and cry, he hung up.

Later, after I had moved into a new apartment, this same man stopped by and told me how sorry he was that he couldn't explain why he'd ended our relationship. He said it as if I knew what he was talking about, but for the life of me, I didn't. *Clue number five.* I accepted his apology on the condition that he help me take up the carpet in my new apartment and also strip the floors. I may have been hurt but I wasn't stupid.

A week or so later a mutual friend mentioned that my ex-boyfriend was gay. I could feel the scales falling from my eyes. Show idea: straight women who date gay men, on the next *Bertice Berry Show.* How could I have been so blind?

He and I got together to talk and he said that when we'd met he'd still been confused about his sexuality. He hadn't really dated many women and felt he hadn't given himself a chance to know if he could be heterosexual. He'd wanted to discover if he was actually gay. I felt like a guinea pig. I told him I thought he'd been unfair to me. Even though he had been uncertain about his sexuality, he should have been up-front with me. I wouldn't have dated him, but I would've been his friend.

I was hurt, but I was even more confused. I'd spent lots of time and energy working on a relationship that I thought was It. I thought of the women who knowingly marry gay men, realizing that the relationship can never be what either of them truly wants or needs. I wondered how and why people could make such a sacrifice.

I realized that this wasn't just about his being straight or gay, it was about people spending their lives with someone who's not right for them. This is easy to do when you don't know who you are or what you need. To find a soul mate you need to know your own soul.

However, my time spent with this first boyfriend was not a loss. The experience helped me to understand who I was and what I wanted. In the process, I'd also realized that there was no particular rush to find what I wanted. My advice to myself was to take my time and make it right.

Rule Four

Look for more.

People tend to select mates who have the one quality they felt was lacking in the previous relationship. Come on, you know you've done this. If the last person you dated was always late or never called, then in the following relationship you look for someone who is always on time and loves to call. This one positive quality often blinds you to other negative ones.

My friend Lola and I laugh about the time when she decided she was tired of dating short men. The next one would be really tall, she proclaimed. He was. But that was all he had going for him. Rule number four is don't settle!

Rule Five

If it's not working, get out quick.

You've seen those horror movies. A family is moving into a haunted house. The real estate agent is played by Vincent Price or Karen Black, the mirrors drip blood, and a spooky voice warns, "Get out."

The husband turns to the wife and says, "Honey, where should we put the sofa?"

Bad relationships are like those horror movies: The signs are there but you ignore them and move in anyway. Don't. Quick, find another house. I always do.

That is one of the reasons my friends think relationships are too short-lived. In truth, most of the time things haven't even evolved to the relationship stage when I stop seeing the person. At first everything seems great. He doesn't do any of those annoying things the last guy did, and life seems to be moving along nicely. But then something happens, and it's over.

I remember one guy in particular. He was a teacher, and I thought we had a lot in common. We were on the phone discussing a talk show I had just taped on Lorena Bobbitt, the woman who severed her husband's penis after he abused and raped her. He surprised me by saying that he couldn't see how a man could rape his wife, since she was obligated to do her duty whenever the husband demanded it. I couldn't believe my ears.

"Do you really mean that?" I asked.

He said of course he did. I told him that our dinner plans for the following evening were canceled. He told me he thought I was being ridiculous, that I was letting my politics affect my personal relationships.

"Please understand," I responded, "that when you hear what I am about to say, it's personal and not political.

"You're stupid!"

I hung up the phone and never spoke to him again.

Rule Six

Never buy shoes when your feet are swollen.

I went from the stress of earning a Ph.D. to getting married without taking a mental-health break. Big mistake.

My ex-husband, Michael, and I had met on a cruise ship where I was doing stand-up comedy and he was playing the piano. He was getting a master's of fine arts in film and also choreography. (No, those weren't clues one, two, and three. Stop stereotyping!)

We had a lot in common, and at first this was enough. We became very close, and then after a year, Michael pronounced out of the blue that we both had callings that could only be realized if we were together. (Good line—don't buy it.)

I thought about his proposal. I prayed and asked God for a sign that would tell me what to do. At the time I was on vacation in Coronado, California, walking on the beach, and when I looked down I found a bus pass with my future husband's full name on it. It was the sign I'd prayed for. Or so I thought. Maybe I should have paid more attention to the concept of "transit," as in "keep moving."

I won't say my relationship with Michael wasn't good to the end, we simply were not equally yoked. It's important to have things in common, but a lifelong bond requires more, like two people should know, understand, and meet one another's needs. It requires that they have similar drives toward meeting their goals, and that they face similar obstacles. A lifetime relationship requires creativity, a degree of ongoing spontaneity, and a lot of hard work. I know this now, but I didn't understand it then.

The marriage only lasted two years.

People lied and said that divorce is like death, like a funeral.

Nope, ain't nobody brought me no food.

My divorce was one of the toughest periods of my life. I never expected anything to hurt so much. Prior to my divorce I had helped friends through breakups, but I hadn't understood why they couldn't get on with their lives, since I hadn't experienced the sense of loss they were feeling firsthand.

Everything reminded me of time that I'd spent with Michael, every song, every book, everything. I couldn't go to the grocery store without thinking, We used to eat food together. I couldn't imagine being without him, but I knew that we couldn't stay together.

So many things had contributed to our breakup. Small things, big things, everything. The fact that I was often on the road doing stand-up comedy didn't help, and the fact that I made more money than he did only made matters worse.

It's a fact of life that our society socializes men to be the primary breadwinners. But men are not the only ones who are brainwashed into thinking this should be the case: Women have the same expectations. People often asked Michael and me if the difference in our salaries created problems between us. We always said no, but then later that night we'd have a big argument about money.

I'd encouraged Michael to cut back on his paying work so he could finish his master's degree, especially since I made enough money to cover our living expenses. The plan was that he'd finish his degree, and then I could take a break from doing 250 comedy dates a year and start fulfilling my own dreams.

But unfortunately, these plans often work better on paper than they do in real life.

Michael said he felt that he wasn't contributing enough to the marriage and, I confess, at times I agreed with him. In addition, he wasn't making much progress on his master's thesis, though I understood that completing a graduate degree was difficult and time-consuming.

Maybe there wasn't enough incentive for him to finish. Usually, one of the reasons you'd want to finish a graduate degree quickly is in order to improve your standard of living. Then once you graduate, you can exchange fellowships and measly stipends for an actual living wage. But since I was earning a good living, our life was already comfortable. We had a loft in Chicago and a lakefront condo in Michigan. What else was there to work for? I probably wouldn't have finished my degree under the same circumstances. The bottom line was that Michael was too comfortable, and that made both of us uncomfortable.

Rule Seven

You gotta be appreciated. You gotta be appreciated. You gotta be appreciated.

I thought part of the problem with our marriage was that Michael didn't recognize all that I was and all that I was doing. It wasn't that I wanted to be put on a pedestal—there's no place to go from there. At the same time, I'd done a whole lot of climbing and I wanted him to appreciate the view.

Michael started coming on the road with me, but that didn't improve the situation. He started taking work that required him to travel, but that didn't work either. It's amazing how couples think that being apart will bring them together. When we separated, we knew immediately that things were coming to an end. And I couldn't figure out why. I'd once been so idealistic about our lives together, but by now I knew that it wasn't going to work.

So here we were, separated. One night around 1 A.M., I found myself missing Michael. *Why was I missing the very person who'd been making me miserable?* I asked myself. But that didn't stop me from calling him and asking him to come over. And this had nothing to do with hormones: It was even more powerful and illogical than that. That night, when I asked him to come over, he came over right away.

I asked him to hold me, but he said he couldn't. He said that something about being there just didn't feel right. He said the apartment no longer felt like his home, that he didn't belong in my life anymore. Michael said he wanted a divorce.

I was crushed. Who did he think he was? I should've been the first one to say it. The pain of divorce was bad enough, but did he also have to tap-dance all over my ego?

I did my best to set aside my ego so that we could make the right decisions and get on with our lives. At first we said some hurtful things to one another, but in the end we made a point of remaining friends.

Rule Eight

Get a prenuptial agreement.

Ours was simple. Whatever we brought to the party was

ours. During the marriage there had been things that had belonged to him, things that had belonged to me, and things that had belonged to us. We kept those lines clear.

Before we got married we didn't have a lot, but we had the potential to make a lot. At that time, we decided we needed a prenuptial not so much to protect ourselves from each other as to protect ourselves from attorneys, who have no emotional investment but can actually stir up a lot of controversy over minor things.

Once we'd decided to divorce, Michael and I got together to decide how to divide our possessions. We determined who got what and what was owed to the other, and we wrote it all down and had it notarized. It was a good thing. As soon as attorneys became involved, they started saying things like, "Well, you should get this," and, "Don't you think he owes you?" It was difficult, but we kept pointing to that notarized paper, which helped us stick to our original agreement.

Throughout this time I was still traveling and doing stand-up comedy. It was strange to have to go out every night and make people laugh when my own heart was broken. I don't know how I did it.

My divorce was final on my thirtieth birthday.

Rule Nine

When it's over, it's over. If you're fat, sing. If you're not, eat something.

Most people know early in a relationship whether or not it can work. When we realize that it won't—even if it hasn't turned into one of those horror movies—we often stay in it anyway because he's cute or it's convenient or because we're afraid of being alone. I'm more afraid of being with someone who's not right for me than of being on my own.

Recently I was seeing a man off and on for about a year. He is probably the most well-rounded, mellow human being I have ever met, a beautiful person who made me feel I had a real sense of balance. So what was wrong with him? you're wondering.

Nothing was wrong with him. The problem was that our lifestyles somehow didn't mesh. He travels all over the world. He gets wonderful jobs all requiring a diverse array of talents, but he only stays in them long enough to earn enough money to move to the next place. In each place he learns a new language, as well as the local culture and customs, which he incorporates into his life. I'd love to go with him, but I don't think I'd be able to fit Fatima, Jabril, and William into my knapsack.

I made the decision to stop seeing him, and he couldn't figure out why. He asked me why we couldn't just enjoy the time we had left together. And I told him because neither of us was terminally ill. I didn't want my emotions to get tangled up in something I knew would end. I'm sure about one thing: I want/need a relationship that will last and this one would not have a chance. It was time to admit it and move on.

I also believe that the things you really need can't reach you if there are obstacles in the way. I've gone through so much to get to the point where I'm happy with who I am, the last thing I need is to start thinking I need a relationship to define myself. A relationship is something a person should want, not desperately need, and that realization can give you tremendous freedom and save a lot of heartache.

I've seen too many women—in my own family, especially—who defined their whole position in life by whether they were involved with a man and by what he could provide for them. I've seen women I've loved and respected trap themselves in horrible situations because they couldn't face the "shame" of breaking off a relationship that everybody else thought was wonderful, or that they thought was at least better than nothing.

Well, honey, plenty of relationships are a lot worse than nothing. I can barely contain myself when I hear something like, "He only hit her *once*." Tell me why he should have hit her at all, I've been known to scream.

I am too sure of myself, too sure of what I have to offer, too sure of what I deserve to ever settle for damaged goods.

Rule Ten

Friendship is forever. Old lovers can be new friends. Old lovers can't be new lovers.

Friends come and go and sometimes come back. I don't do this with lovers. Once you're gone, so is that love. I might be missing something, but I don't want to relive the same thing that didn't work the first time over and over again. Let's face it: When love is involved, we tend to remember more of the good than the bad.

This nostalgia is necessary; it's part of feeling the hurt and then letting it go. But it also makes it easy to romanticize whatever it was that failed. I've had old boyfriends tell me that they've changed and that they can make it work this time. I say, Save it for someone who hasn't been through what we've been through together. Move on.

My friend Peaches will say to men she's dumping, "Think of how good you'll be for your new girlfriend."

When love is gone, it's gone. Friendship is forever. That's how it should be.

Love Mentors

When I was growing up, my mother was without a partner, but even so, I was surrounded by all kinds of loving relationships. I haven't given up on love; the examples of many of my friends tell me that caring couples are not a thing of the past, that they have what I've come to know as true love. Love that is sought after, obtained, and maintained. And it's comfortable.

My high school music teacher and his wife, Leander and Lucille Morris, were a terrific example. They called themselves Cil and Lee. (Cil and Lee. It always sounded funny to me, like a hardware store or something.) They'd finish each other's sentences, and even each other's thoughts. You never heard them actually argue. It was more like quiet reconciliation.

Lee would phone home and say, "Cil, I'm bringing home some of my students. Do we have any food?"

"Of course, Lee," Cil would reply.

Now, in case you missed it, that was an argument. What they were thinking was more like this:

Cil, I know you don't like it when I call at the last minute, but it's better than me not calling at all. So I'm calling to tell you that I'm bringing home some kids, and you need to cook something. Now do you need anything?

To which she's thinking: You know I don't like you calling at the last minute, bringing them loud kids in my house, and besides, we never spend any time together alone. No, you don't have to bring anything home because I'm prepared. I'm always prepared, 'cause I know that you are going to do this and because your students are my kids, too, and I love them.

But Cil and Lee never said any of that. All they had to say was "I'm bringing them" and "I'll be ready."

There was also Mr. and Mrs. Thompson, my best friend Tia's mom and dad. Now they could argue. Hot, sassy arguments.

"Why didn't you tell me?"

"I did tell you, Harry."

"Oh, never mind then."

Throughout any given meal, Mr. and Mrs. T. would communicate without saying a thing. One time, we were eating corn on the cob. Mr. T. had just been served his corn when he took it and raised it over his head. Without a word Mrs. T. got up, went to the refrigerator, got the butter, and put it on Mr. T.'s corn.

Now, I had just come home from college and was learning a lot about women's rights and how far we had *not* come. This corn-buttering exchange had probably happened before, but I hadn't noticed it. So for me it was amplified. I looked at Mrs. T. and asked her why Mr. T. couldn't get his own butter.

They just looked at each other and smiled a very secret smile. Then Mrs. T. politely informed me that she could scratch her own back, but Mr. T. always did it for her and she never had to ask. I didn't say anything else 'cause I knew this back-scratching thing really meant something else and I didn't want to go there. There was no philosophy or ideology that could explain their love.

My pastor and his wife, the Reverend Mr. and Mrs. Rainey, were called Pop Pop and Nan Nan by practically everybody in the entire city of Wilmington. But they had much more interesting names for each other. Names like Strawberry Shortcake and Peach Cobbler. Just hearing them talk to one another could make you hungry.

She was married to him and he was married to the church. Because of their dedication, I have not dated, nor do I ever intend to date, a man of the cloth. I want a man who loves God, but I'd like most of his time to be spent with me. (I'm not selfish, just honest.)

Pop Pop understood Nan Nan's sacrifice and indulged her in things that seemed frivolous to me. He'd spend hours helping her decide which shade of yellow shoes went best with her favorite yellow dress. He'd hang the same wallpaper over and over till the patterns matched to Nan Nan's satisfaction.

I knew Pop Pop had other things to do, but they'd complete these chores together as if they were newlyweds. After forty-five years of marriage, Pop Pop and Nan Nan were still the perfect couple.

Leo and Melody Jackson, my brother/sister/friends, display for each other a passionate love that all couples should have. They're both heavier than they were when they first met in college, but whenever one enters the room, they both act as if they are seeing each other for the first time and can't wait to be together.

"Man, my wife looks good," Leo says out loud.

"Stop it, Leo," Melody replies.

After thirteen years of marriage they're still playful. At times their public displays of affection make me blush. Leo, a Pentecostal preacher, will be at the dinner table talking about food.

"Hmmm, baby, these thighs are good, but not as good as the ones I had last night." Leo and Melody are grinning like Cheshire cats, then one of the children exclaims, "Daddy, we didn't have chicken last night."

They've had their troubles, as all young couples do. The financial burden of their large family is at times trying, but they remember why they're together and keep on loving each other. They go on dates and giggle like guilty teenagers when they get home. Their house is full of prayers, music, laughter, and love.

Ring and Ernestine Williams, my friend Rhonda's parents, are proof that if you can travel together, you can live together. When it comes to getting lost on a trip, Ring is the stereotypical male. He won't ask for directions. Instead, he tries to get within the general location of wherever he's going. "If you can get in the general vicinity of a place," he says, "then you can find it." Rhonda respectfully asks, "Then where are we now, Daddy?"

Her mother replies, "We're in the general vicinity."

They don't yell and scream like many couples do. They discuss. These discussions sometimes last for weeks. And when they come to an agreement, they both act as if they hadn't moved from their original positions. They compromise without ever admitting it.

Peaches Anderson is one of those single women who will always find love. I met her in my graduate program, and if it had not been for the fact that we were two Black women in a predominantly White environment, we would *not* have been friends.

Peaches can rub you the wrong way. She's loud and assertive and cusses like a sailor. But once you get past all that, you realize that she's got a zest for life like no one else you've ever met. She says her mother was the most loving woman who ever lived, but she died young. Peaches promised her mother and herself that she'd live life to the fullest. No one could top her at that. Peaches loves love. "Shit, it's spring," she says. "I need to be in love."

If her boyfriend looks at her funny, she knows she can find another one, "'cause life is way too motherfucking short." She'll love one guy because of his hands and another because of his feet. Then she'll love a third just because *he* needs to be in love. "Yes, motherfucker, I love you, too," Peaches says.

I marvel at how this ordinary woman always finds love, and then I realize that the reason is simple: She's got a lot of love to give.

Love Unspoken

In the Black community, as in all communities, there are those loves that are not openly discussed. Loves that must remain secret or unspoken.

I have often wrestled with my own attitudes and beliefs concerning homosexual relationships. I wrestle with my Pentecostal upbringing, which not only fails to recognize these relationships but also views them as an abomination in the eyes of God. But these relationships are real, they are here, and they, too, have had a positive influence on my perceptions of love.

Unfortunately, I can't name these people. It would be too much pressure on them. I've watched gay couples who have been together for years. Too often, their families refer to the significant other as "my son's special friend," or they don't acknowledge them at all. They argue like other couples, but rarely do they have the necessary resources made available to help them when their relationship is in trouble, and so they end up having to attend a version of heterosexual marriage counseling or just letting things fizzle out. Sometimes these couples make it. Sometimes they don't. But when they do, they still can't be entirely free.

Because they so often can't openly display their affection for each other, these couples have made an art out of the significant gesture, the silent signal that communicates the bond between them. They learn to know one another and to recognize that they have more in common than their gender alone. They share the same dreams and desires and they intend to get there together.

Who am I to call it wrong or to deny their existence? If love is love, then they surely have it.

What This Woman Really Wants

I usually walk through my life feeling content with work and the ability to think clearly, feeling that the absence of a long-term lover is not a big concern. But then, when I take a good look at the loves around me, I know that I want that in my life, too. I want the understanding between Cil and Lee, and Mr. and Mrs. T.; I want the balance between Nan Nan and Pop Pop, the passion between Leo and Melody, and the diligent and loving compromises being struck by Ring and Ernestine. I yearn for the ability to be in love with being in love like Peaches, and the tenaciousness of my gay friends who stay together against the odds.

I want my life to be balanced and in sync with that of another person. But finding this love is not a preoccupation, it's dessert. My life as it is, is the full-course meal. But God knows I love sweets.

When it's right, it's right. I won't let my hormones, three fatherless children, or my loneliness force me into anything. People spend their single lives trying to be married, and their married lives wishing they were single. When the time is right for me and the man is right for the time, I want to be prepared to recognize it.

When she was single, my friend Terry Early-Davis said that when she finally found her husband, she felt the need to apologize to him for all the tough times he'd gone through. She said that she knew all his trials were really for her, that they had helped mold him into the man she had prayed for.

I, too, am being made into what God has called me to be and into what my true love needs. I also know that there is some poor brother out there going through hell. Eventually we'll find each other.

MORE OF WHAT WE ARE

Hello it's me
Tapping at the door of your heart
Don't let me bother you
I could come back when it's more
More of what we want
More of what we need
More of what we are
We are like two lost lovers, searching
To find our way home
Home is where I find you
Sitting, waiting, watching, praying
Listening at the door of your heart
It's me knocking at the door to your soul
It's you watching from the window of matched loneliness
Wondering if I'll ever come back when it's
More of what we want
More of what we need
More of what we are, like two lost lovers,
Lost.

Every now and again I find the need to reevaluate my life to determine what I truly need and what I can do without. I do this with clothes, furniture, and people. Sometimes I feel as if I'm carrying baggage that doesn't belong to me, and it's slowing me down. I might meet people who seem great for me, until I discover that they're not who I thought they were. Maybe it's me. Maybe I've changed and they're the same.

Sometimes you want a person to change on your timetable even when you know they can't. Trying to change someone always backfires. The best thing you can do for yourself is to stay on your own path, moving forward.

If you happen to see my tracks and want to join me on the journey, I'd be happy for the company.

CHAPTER FIVE

Education: Getting It

I always heard that White people were smart. Best thing that ever happened to me was going to school with them. I called home and said, "Mom, they got dumb ones, too."

I can't ever remember not wanting to read. I've always loved learning. I'm sure that it's one of those things that has been passed down to me.

Education is the single most important avenue for change and advancement. More than any other institution in society, education can truly change your life. More than family, more than work, even more than religion.

Education has always been important to my family. Unfortunately, it's not something they were all able to get, even though they are all bright and informed people. This sounds like a contradiction, but it's not. There are really two types of education. Formal, which is taught in classrooms via textbooks, and informal, which is passed on through verbal and nonverbal communication. An informal education is the learning that just happens when you simply listen to your elders or when a tree falls in the woods. And, yes, it makes a sound even though you aren't there to hear it, because common sense should tell you that the whole world doesn't revolve around you.

Learning happens when you stop long enough to watch a bird land, wonder what kind it is, and then go and find out. Learning comes from meditation, prayer, and exercise. It can happen via word of mouth, words of wisdom, or words from books that no one made you read. Learning happens naturally and miraculously.

When *The Bertice Berry Show* started to run, people treated me as if I'd come out of nowhere. "Who is this woman and why does she have a talk show?" they said.

Reporters bombarded me with the same questions over and over. "Do we really need another talk show?" and "What gives you the right to have one?" What they were really thinking was, How come you got a talk show and I didn't? One reporter went as far as to imply that I hadn't earned a Ph.D. Well, nah, nah nah nah nah, nah.

What these people had overlooked was that besides having become one of the most successful stand-up comediennes in the country, I had paid my dues, and lots of 'em, for a long time before I ever went on the air. Everyone has to pay dues; some people should owe more. I had spent years honing my craft as a performer and a perceptive observer of social phenomena.

If someone had offered me that show five years earlier, there is absolutely no way I would have been able to do it. I was learning, preparing myself, if not specifically for a talk show, then for something that would put me in front of the public, for cutting to the heart of matters, and for asking questions that led to the truth.

I tell everybody who'll listen—and especially those who won't but need to—that as important as it is to dream, dreams don't mean much if you don't take the next step to try to make your dreams a reality. This means hard work, hard work, and more hard work. There's no way around it.

The academic phrase that applies here is *deferred gratification.* It means putting off what you want until you've gotten what you need. When you've already worked hard for a long time, it can be easy to be distracted by something that promises a sudden payoff. But that sudden payoff isn't achieving your dream, it's settling for something short of what you really need. It won't make you happy for long, and it can set you back in your race to the real finish.

One of my mother's favorite lines when I was growing up was "Fifty dollars is not a down payment for a Cadillac." Her point was that, for us, fifty dollars was a rare thing. If we could save it up, it shouldn't be spent on something we couldn't afford or maintain—and didn't really need. If it was all we had, there were obviously more important needs. Dreams, however, should never be deferred. They should be those ever-present blueprints for the real things.

There are countless wonderful dreams that people can have, from being a nurse's aide to being president of the United States. The paths that lead us to those dreams are all unique to the people who follow them. The path that we must all take is the path of education, both formal and informal.

When you seek out new ideas, new experiences, new people, new places—whether it's at Howard or Ace Technical School—you make your mind bigger. You acquire more information, more wisdom, to apply in any situation you confront. This is true in your home, in your church, in your job, and especially in your dreams.

You're not going to accumulate knowledge and experience without taking a few knocks. You're going to meet people who will discourage you, you're going to have to make some choices about what's important, you're going to encounter some things that in the end you will reject because they're false.

You're going to have to be ready to meet those tough times

with determination, with a passion for what you're going after, and you're going to have to find people who will say, "Yes, you should do this, and you can."

Believe me. 'Cause I've done all that.

The Education of Bertice Berry: A Short Course

My sister Chris taught me to read and write before I ever entered kindergarten. In school, I was always an eager student. In the summers, because we liked the real thing so much, my cousin Robin and I set up our own pretend school. As soon as I knew what college was, I wanted to go there.

By my first year or so of high school, I wasn't acting like a person on her way to college. But with some encouragement from the kind people every child needs, I eventually renewed my determination to get an education. Despite the jeering from the sidelines, I not only got into college, I also received a scholarship from a benefactor that enabled me to attend Jacksonville University.

At JU, determined not only to graduate but to be an exceptional student, I worked like a dog, making up for all the members of my family who had never had this opportunity. More wonderful people kept me excited about learning, got me over an occasional fit of pique because my family didn't understand what I was doing, and encouraged me to go to grad school.

I graduated from JU with honors and a commendation for being the most outstanding student in my class. From there I entered the master's program at Kent State University in Ohio. It was like starting all over: I felt uneducated and years behind my classmates. I compensated by working like a slave from can't see to can't see and was rewarded by the praise of professors, who told me that I ought to push on for my Ph.D.

Nothing can describe the pressure and the work getting a Ph.D. involved. I got mine in sociology, studying Black-on-Black discrimination, or colorism, the preferential treatment of people on the basis of their skin color.

During my graduate years, I paid my way as a researcher and as a teacher. Through teaching I discovered my ability to entertain as well as educate; a harmless attempt to win fifty dollars in a comedy competition had fateful results.

The rest is herstory.

Of course, it wasn't that simple. *Simple?* It was hell. Along the way I heard all kinds of people tell me that I didn't have what it takes, including an ideal family life. I traded a small, tight community of people like me for a vast, competitive world of people very unlike me. I faced racism, blatant and more blatant. And I struggled with doubt.

As time went by, that small voice that had always been saying "You can do it" grew louder. I knew that I had a love of learning, the determination to succeed, the encouragement of terrific people, and the support of a God who had promised me that She would always leave me a path up and out.

See Bertice Read
Read, Bertice, Read

When I learned that many enslaved African brothers and sisters were not allowed to read and were punished and sometimes even put to death for reading, I decided to read for them.

At first, I was an angry reader. I'd get on the bus to go downtown with my mother and I'd read out loud. I'd always sit in the front, pointing out that someone had earned this right for me. I'd look directly in the face of some White person and would practically shout, "See Spot run." With a big scowl on my face I'd go on, "Run, Spot, run!"

For me, reading was and is a revolutionary act. It expands my mind and gives me the necessary tools for the revolution of my spirit, the revolution of my mind, and the revolution of society.

It bothers me that people don't read more. I've met college students who say they don't like to read. This is like saying you don't like to pee. You have to do it. Sometimes you don't want to, but the urge builds up. You know what I mean. Like late at night, the bathroom's just a few steps away, but it feels like miles. You finally get up to take that long journey, and when you do it, you swear that it's the best thing that's ever happened to you. Reading gives you that same kind of reward.

Recently I was discussing a book idea with a Black woman who declared that our race couldn't afford any more bad books.

"Twenty-four dollars and ninety-five cents is way too much for my people to pay for bad books," she said.

"Well, I think twenty-four ninety-five is pretty cheap for hours of entertainment and mental exercise."

"Yeah, that's true. But if our people have to spend that much on a book, then it should be a good one."

"I agree, but if our people can afford two hundred dollars for a pair of running shoes, and they don't even run, then I think twenty-four ninety-five, good or bad, is still an excellent buy."

I once saw a homeless man lying outside in the cold on a

heat vent. He was reading a book. I thought of all the people who had homes but not books. And here was this man with no home and few possessions. He chose to have a book.

Chose to read, chose to learn, chose to dream.

No Substitutions, Please

There are some misinformed people who will tell you that you can get by without education and experience. They say that just being a good soul is all it takes. Ignorance is not bliss; it's imprisonment. Get out!

A visiting preacher at my church once thundered, "You don't need a degree in *the*-ology, what you need is a little *knee*-ology." My pastor, Pop Pop, got up as quick as he could to remind us all that the Scriptures also told us to study. But I'm afraid that some of my friends took the other message to heart.

Many of my church friends attended my high school. At lunchtime, we all gathered at the same table and witnessed about the goodness of God—to each other. Some of them spent so much time putting God first that they didn't have much time for school or homework.

In church they'd testify about how they knew that God would help them on their exams. But in school, they failed miserably. Pop Pop would tell us that God could only bring back into our memory that which was already there. He reminded us that spiritual excellence required academic excellence.

And, yes, for a while I made the same mistake, just as I'd once used my service to God as an excuse to avoid dating. But in both cases, I learned that God works in mysterious ways Her wonders to perform—but you better work!

Get the Bad News Over With

You already know enough about my home life to realize that it wasn't the ideal environment. Some other factors also conspired against my success.

Not the least of these was the attitude of *some* of my teachers. I entered high school with a few chips on my shoulder. I was an overweight girl from an abusive, alcoholic home, and thanks to the fact that I had used my church as a refuge against an oppressive world, I walked around with an air of religious superiority. My assignments were sloppy and often late. I acted up in classes or cut them. I was a card-carrying member of the "Who you looking at?" club.

Pierre Samuel duPont High School was then a predominantly Black school. It had been all-White until an influx of Blacks into the neighborhood in the sixties had caused White flight.

Many of the teachers who had been at P.S. (as we called it) a long time often reminded us of the school's "better days." One teacher actually told me she never expected anything from her Black students. She boldly professed that we, like our parents, couldn't be educated; the situation was hopeless. My classmates and I complained among ourselves, but we didn't take our complaints anywhere. We made the mistake of internalizing someone else's stupidity.

But in my sophomore year of high school, we had to declare whether we were vocational or college prep students. Faced with a choice, I didn't even have to think about it. I came out of the college closet.

When I announced my decision to head for college, one of

life's many naysayers tried to dissuade me. I don't want to use his name because people can change and they should have the opportunity to do so. Let's just call him Scum Sucking Dog.

This poor excuse for a teacher laughed in my face at the news that I dared to think I was college material. He was the one who told me no college would accept me, and if they did, they'd send me home as soon as they got a look at me.

Scum Sucking Dog's words were still in my head as I headed off to college. My entire trip from Wilmington to Jacksonville University in Florida was filled with fear. I was praying nonstop.

A kindly old White couple in the seats next to me thought I was some kind of psychiatric patient confronting my fear of flying. I started to tell them my life story, and before I knew it, I was blabbing like a talk-show guest. They smiled and told me not to worry. They told me that college was a new place where I could start out fresh; any problems I had at home could remain there. If I was a good student before, then I'd be a great one at JU.

This couple's random act of kindness was enough to take my mind off Scum Sucking Dog, at least until we landed. I rode from the airport to JU in a van full of White, really White, students. I just knew my name was not going to be on the list of new students, that my being there was some kind of mistake.

We arrived at the school and I saw people unloading cars the likes of which I had seen only on TV. *Please let my name be on the list.* The registration line was long, and it was unbelievably hot and humid. My fear only grew. *Please let my name be on the list.* By the time I got to the front of the line I was so dizzy I thought I'd pass out.

"Are you okay?" the woman behind the desk asked.

"Please let my name be on the list," I blurted out.

"Okay. What is your name?"

"Bertice Berry," I replied a little too quickly.

"Berry, Berry, Berry, Bertrice. Here it is."

I didn't care how she pronounced it as long as it was there. I asked her to show me so I could see for myself. "Berry, Bertice. Room 418B." I smiled as if I were stupid. If I'd been a numbers player, I would have played 418, boxed and straight.

I was in. My name was on the list and nothing that Scum Sucking Dog or any other negative person had said would ever matter. I decided right then that I would stay on the list and be on every other important list there was: the dean's list, the president's list, and the graduation list. I was going to get a college degree and I'd make everyone proud, even those who said I wouldn't make it.

People were counting on me. I was there for a purpose, not only for me, but for my ancestors, who had yearned to be free and educated. I was there for Caroline and Annie and John Henry Freeman. I was there for those who'd died for my right to be free. I would read for Chris, who had put her education on hold for me. I would study for my brothers and sisters, and for my mother, whose dreams had been deferred. I was in and nothing would ever change that.

Not in Academia! I'm Shocked and Appalled

Before I left for JU, Nan Nan had warned me that Jacksonville had some of the reddest necks in the country. The town sure did. I was cursed in grocery stores, and people threw things at me from moving cars. The university was much better, and yet . . .

I was often singled out because I was Black. Anytime a topic came up concerning race, poverty, crime, and almost anything dysfunctional, I was looked to as the "local expert." My class-mates, and at times even my professors, made me feel as if I had written *The Farmer's Almanac of Social Problems.* "Why do people steal?" someone might ask. "Let's ask Bertice, she should know."

Sometimes things weren't so subtle. I was called names ranging from nigger to spear chucker. My neck was moving so much I had whiplash. You should know by now that I had to confront these situations head-on.

During my sophomore year one student continually made derogatory comments about Black students. She'd say these things to her friends loudly enough for everyone to hear. "Why do they let the jigaboos in here? They can't even read."

Sometimes, when a group of Black students came close to her, she'd say things like, "Do you guys smell anything? Something smells like a dead raccoon." We confronted her and told her that she was offensive. She acted as if she didn't know what we were talking about and dismissed our accusations.

Some of my friends wanted to take her down by the river and give her a good butt-kicking. We decided against it (deferred gratification, y'all), realizing that we'd be the ones to get kicked out of school. She'd be the winner. We thought about how to get back at her and eventually came up with a plan that everyone liked.

The JU dorms were full of palmetto bugs. *Palmetto bug* is just a nice way of saying huge, hairy, man-eating cockroach. We decided to collect as many of these roaches as possible. Some died, but we kept them anyway.

I worked at the campus post office and had access to every-one's mailbox. This woman's box was high enough up that she couldn't see directly into it. She had to open it and grope inside for the contents.

I waited until she came for her mail and, when no one was

looking, poured our collection of roaches into her mailbox. When she opened it, she got the surprise of her narrow-minded little life. Her hand and her hair were full of roaches. When she screamed, one went into her mouth. (And I was thinking, Aren't roaches a delicacy somewhere?)

My friends had been waiting around to watch the excitement. They gave her the old "we know where you live" look. She never bothered us again.

Another young woman from a tiny town in upstate New York referred to all Blacks as niggers. She did this right to our faces. She lived in my dorm. In the showers she stared at me as if I were someone in a bad women's prison movie.

I confronted her and she said, "How come your breasts are black?"

"*I'm* black."

"I thought they'd be whiter, like the palms of your hands and the soles of your feet."

"No, stupid, you have me confused with the orangutan and your mother," I shouted.

She burst into tears and said she hadn't ever known any Black people before. She hadn't even been allowed to watch them on TV. Her father had called Blacks niggers and she thought this was the appropriate term. I corrected her and loaned her some books. To her credit, she read them and went to the library for more. She never became my close friend, but she said that she was changed.

Campus racism didn't just come from my peers. At times I had to confront professors about comments they made or their unfair grading systems. Discrimination in the classroom was always difficult to deal with, but there were procedures to be followed and an administration that was sympathetic and responsive.

One professor graded me much lower than I felt I deserved. My friends told me they'd had problems, too. We spoke to a faculty member, who agreed to talk with this professor; his behavior only got worse.

The professor who'd been helpful wanted to go to the university president. I told her that my friends and I would try reason one more time. This time all of my Black friends went to see this professor. They didn't say anything, but all thirty of them just stood there as I explained that I felt my race had affected his ability to grade fairly. He stuttered and coughed and changed my grade.

We gained faith in official channels because of one incident in particular. JU had a large international student body, most of whom were wealthy. They soon found out, however, that their ethnic differences denied them the privileges of their wealth. Students came from all over the world, and we had a sizable group from Iran.

This was during the Carter administration when Americans were being held hostage in Teheran. A group of White students demonstrated for the expulsion of all Iranian students from JU. Dr. Frances Kinnie, the university president, heard about this and went to confront the mob.

No student would ever be removed from JU because of his or her race or nationality, Dr. Kinnie informed them, but any student could be removed for hatred and bigotry. Everyone knew she meant it.

Part of the Gang

Kent State seemed like an enormous change, but in many ways it wasn't. The school was huge compared to JU: twenty thousand students versus five thousand. But it was just as White. With the exception of the black squirrels that ran around the campus, the place was a virtual blizzard. In my early comedy routines, I joked that the squirrels had been imported to meet affirmative-action quotas.

When I decided to move into the doctoral program, one of my professors told me that he felt that I wasn't the right kind of student. This surprised me, since my decision had been made with much encouragement from some of the department's leading scholars. I asked him why.

He told me that good grades weren't all that I needed to be in the program. He mumbled something about "being part of the gang." I wasn't exactly sure what he meant, but I knew that I wasn't part of the gang. My mother had always told me to stay away from them.

I spoke with Dr. Elizabeth Mullins, with whom I was doing research. She told me to get over it. She said that there would always be people who would never accept Blacks or women as part of the intelligentsia. If I intended to prove them wrong, the best thing to do was to stop bellyaching and get on about the business of the Ph.D.

When I started work on my dissertation on colorism, I had to confront the most profound ignorance about my subject. Some of my committee members wanted to use a little color swatch to measure the skin color of the respondents.

Can you imagine me holding a paint chip up to someone's face? "Get out of here, girl. I know what color I am!" I actually had to do a sample study to prove that Black people know what color their skin is.

I had problems finding an apartment in Kent because nobody wanted to rent to a Black woman. I was reporting landlords to the housing authorities left and right. When one of my professors heard about my trials, he said, "I can't believe this is happening to you. Do you want me to call them up and tell them you're a good Black?"

Whom could I report him to?

Under the guise of rigorous academic standards, a member of my dissertation committee jerked me around mercilessly. One day he called me in to tell me that it wasn't necessary to write *he/she* since *he* was universally understood to mean both. So I dropped *he* and used *she* everywhere. Then he called me in to tell me that it wasn't necessary to capitalize *Black* and *White*. So I stopped capitalizing *white*.

But I gradually tired of the game and called him up and told him, "You are no longer *necessary* to my committee."

Even after I had defended my dissertation, it continued. As people stood around congratulating me, another professor came up and said, "You know Asians have this color thing, too. It's true, and the Koreans are the worst."

It still goes on. From store clerks who won't show me something because they think I can't afford it to entertainment executives who tell me that I don't know my place. (Is it the field or the kitchen, massa?)

But as crazy as it makes me, it doesn't stop me. Education was my right and my desire. I learned to pursue it despite these legions of idiots. Sometimes what's meant to be bad can turn out good.

Wait, It Gets Better

It's more than I can do to name all the people who have encouraged me and given me a boost. But some of them also taught me lessons that have truly stayed with me.

It was Chris who first told me that knowledge was the power and the key to success no matter how I defined it. She was always trying to add some knowledge to our lives. She even taught us table manners by taking us to a diner up the street where we ordered toasted cheese sandwiches as if they were filet mignon and used flatware as if it were silver at the Duchess of Windsor's table.

My elementary school teachers never waited till February to teach us about Black history. It was part of every lesson we had. We learned about Pedro Alonzo Niño, Christopher Columbus's Black navigator on his first voyage, and the Native Americans who had been living here quite happily before they were "discovered."

Our classes were always being visited by guest speakers, who taught us that Black people could be artists, chemical engineers, or anything that we wanted to be. These were living examples of the possibilities that education brought, and they were exciting to us.

When I entered high school with my *slight* attitude problem, it was Karen Denton, my English teacher, who saw and believed in my potential. She'd take my deliberately sloppy papers and actually read them. (Of course, this was her job, but too often teachers don't do their jobs.)

I was testing this White Midwesterner to see if she really cared about her Black students. She had me figured out from day one. She moved me to her advanced-placement English (APE) course and suggested that teachers in other departments do the same.

Despite the fact that I always flounced into her class late, Miss Denton didn't give up on me. She kept me interested in what we were doing. Her outrageous teaching methods awakened my academic curiosity. She taught us Shakespeare and encouraged us to rewrite it in our vernacular. She taught us to understand it and, by having us translate it, made sure we really knew it and saw its power.

Mrs. Atlanta Brown, our high school librarian, had a drawl as Southern as her name. She saw past my fear of being labeled a librarian-loving nerd. She recommended books that she thought I'd enjoy and encouraged my excitement. She never seemed to notice that I thought I was too cool to even say "thank you."

Instead of flunking me for skipping his Spanish class nearly every day, Jesus Prado let the strength of my test scores govern my grade. Besides, he told me, "You are a bigger problem in the classroom than when you are not here." I had the grace to be embarrassed.

My creative writing teacher, Bruce Laird, was one of the White teachers who had been at P.S. in its "better days." But he felt that the "Black presence" had actually made an improvement in the school. He loved our spirit and creativity. He directed us toward Black writers like Richard Wright and James Baldwin. He got us tickets to local plays and even took a group of us to New York to see Stephanie Mills in *The Wiz*.

There was this fourteen-year-old girl singing loud enough for us to hear it in the last row of the last balcony. I wanted to be on that stage. I didn't think it would ever be possible, but I didn't throw the dream out. I hid it in the secret place in my soul.

P.S. duPont High School's greatest gift to me was Leander Morris, my music teacher. He took a room of rowdy misfits and turned us into a choir. He taught us to be not only good performers but decent human beings as well. "Someone is always waiting in the wings," he said. "They may be better than you, they may be worse, but they are there."

Mr. Morris knew the power of travel to open up young minds. We went on tour to places as far-flung as Bermuda and Detroit. We were in Detroit when the news came over the radio that the King of Rock and Roll had died. "Lord," Mr. Morris said, "I'm sure gonna miss Little Richard."

My guidance counselor, Mr. Pinkett, worked with Miss Denton to encourage my college dreams. They got me into Upward Bound, a program to help underprivileged students explore the possibility of college. Mr. Ed Morris, the Upward Bound director, was a dignified Black man who helped to make the fantasy of college a reality. All the Upward Bound instructors were electrifying. They stoked our desire for education and helped us complete the applications.

Bertice Gets a Choice

With the help of Upward Bound, Miss Denton, Mr. Morris, and Mr. Pinkett, I knew that I was going to college. The choice of one was dizzying. All the catalogs looked the same. The covers always had four friends, smiling happily. One of these friends was always Black. When I'd open up the catalogs, though, there was only a sea of White faces.

My friend Tia Thompson was also going to college. She, too, had been told that she was not college material, but her family ignored this advice. Mr. and Mrs. Thompson supported me as well, intellectually and physically. After we had been evicted from that house on Gordon Street, I had moved from my family's temporary housing into their home. "You spend so much time here anyway," they said laughing. I loved them for it.

Tia wanted to be a musician and applied to Norfolk State

College in Virginia, a "historically Black" college. I applied there as well, along with another predominately White college.

Completely unbeknownst to me, one of the guidance counselors had also sent my application to Jacksonville University. When the acceptance came, I was excited but confused. The counselor who'd sent my application in explained it. She told me that JU was a good school and that she thought a new environment would be good for me.

My confusion only grew when I was accepted at Norfolk State and the other school where I had applied. I decided to wait and see what the financial aid packages would be like, since I was in no position to go to any of the schools without some help.

I was in Scum Sucking Dog's class when Mr. Pinkett called me out. A few minutes later I was dancing back through the door yelling, "I'm going to college." Arfy-boy just shook his head.

Mr. Pinkett had told me that a wealthy White man who was a friend of a JU professor wanted to sponsor a student, preferably a Black one, who without financial support would sink but with it could go far. My application had been on the desk for review when he called the school, and I had been selected. This was the first time I ever heard of Terry Evenson.

I had worked all my life for this moment and here it was: the Ability to Choose. I cried. I finally had a choice to make, and it was terrifying. This is why most folks stay in a familiar situation instead of choosing a different path.

I tried to get advice from my family and friends. I went to my mother and asked for her opinion. This was not something she was accustomed to. My brothers had both enlisted in the Army and neither had asked for her permission. Portia had turned down dance scholarships and already given birth to her first baby. She hadn't consulted my mom either.

When I asked my mom what she thought, she said, "It's up to you, it's your life. Just don't bring no babies in here."

"Uh, thanks," I said, and left.

Nan Nan and Pop Pop told me to pray, and I did. Miss Denton told me she thought I was ready for the challenge of Jacksonville. Tia's parents agreed, but reminded me to pray. I prayed and prayed and prayed. When I didn't feel I was getting an answer, I asked God for a sign.

After a week of trying to decide, I realized that maybe God was reminding me that God helps those who help themselves. I called both Norfolk and JU from Mr. Pinkett's office, hoping to get some kind of vibe. The people at JU were helpful and said that they were looking forward to seeing me.

When I called Norfolk, I had to go through several people before I got the one I needed. Then, in the middle of the conversation, the phone went dead.

Mr. Pinkett told me to call them back. Tia was also present and she looked at him and said, "She doesn't have to. She just got her sign."

I started making plans to go to Jacksonville. If I was ready for college, I was ready to go there.

More Help for the Hopeful

Once I was on the path, others helped keep me walking in the right direction.

Norm Pollock never got over the fact that I insisted on calling him "Mr. Pollock." "Call me Norm," he'd say, to which I replied, "I wasn't raised like that."

I took my first sociology class with Mr. Pollock. He came running in late, carrying an oversize bookbag. He held up the bag and said, "This is *my* bag. I can throw it if I want to."

And he did, right across the room.

He ran and picked it up and began to stroke it as if it were a hurt puppy. "I can stroke this bag if I want," he continued. He went on to illustrate that things were things and they could belong to people. But people, on the other hand, were individuals with feelings and thoughts of their own. These thoughts, however, were all connected to the other people around them.

"The self is social," he proclaimed.

I was spellbound. For weeks I pondered the fact that I would never be alone because, in some way, everyone I had ever met was with me. I started making a "Who Am I?" list. On it I included the names of the people I knew, the books I'd read, and every event I could remember as having had an impact.

Nan Nan, Pop Pop, Mr. Morris, Mr. and Mrs. T. I walked around in a state of philosophical bliss. *Mom, Chris, Myrna, Portia, Kevin, Brent, Tanya.* I shared my excitement with my friends, who joked that I should be committed. *"Swing Low." "I Want You Back." "Someday We'll Be Together."* They told me that I was getting in too deep and that I ought to come back to the surface. *"Bet You by Golly Wow." "Reasons." "If You Believe."* I realized that I was going a bit overboard, but my sociological imagination was awake and on fire.

Pillow Talk

Though Terry Evenson was generously helping me, I was determined to carry as much of my own load as possible. I became a resident assistant in the dorms to reduce my housing costs (and get a private bathroom). Doing so put me in touch with Sally Myers.

Somehow she was the only professor at JU I could call by her first name. In addition to being director of the women's dormitories, Sally taught art therapy. I was excited by the idea of combining art with healing and enrolled in her class.

When Sally announced an assignment called "pillow fantasy" and told us to bring a pillow to the next class, we all thought that she had reached new heights in her already outrageous teaching techniques. When we arrived that day, she told us to stretch out on the floor. Then she turned out the lights and coaxed us to relax. I was thinking, Free schools and crazy White people.

Sally told us to visualize our ideal creation. It could be anything: a painting, a song, a performance. Her only request was that it be incredible.

I started thinking that maybe Sally wasn't so crazy and that I could get into this. I began to imagine a project where I'd combine information with entertainment. I would have this great delivery. I'd be funny and informative. There would be an audience that would also participate. We would find solutions to their problems through humor, song, and education.

I got lost in the fantasy. After about twenty minutes, Sally instructed us to return from the fantasy but remember it. I expected her to tell us to share the fantasies we'd had. Instead, she told us that we should write an outline of what we'd imagined.

We all wrote furiously, and at the end of class, none of us were finished. Then Sally informed us that what we had written would be our final exam; we had to realize our fantasy. "But it was just a fantasy," someone complained. "Yeah," another student chimed in, "my idea is too complex to produce."

Sally smiled the world's biggest grin and said, "If you can imagine it, you can create it."

At the end of the semester, students brought in some of the most amazing work I'd seen: self-portraits, sets of dishes. My presentation couldn't be carried in a bag.

I organized the class to sit as if they were members of a television audience. I brought in my friends, who performed beautiful music and joined my panel to discuss relevant topics. It was a combination of daytime talk show and late-night variety show. It was a big hit.

I forgot about this experience until I signed the deal for *The Bertice Berry Show*. When I remembered, I marveled at how profoundly Sally had helped me to anticipate what I was going to do years before I had any idea I was going to do it.

A Little Extracurricular Support

Not everyone who strengthened and inspired me at JU was a teacher. I got support from two very different quarters.

On the one hand was the staff of JU. Everyone from the janitors and cafeteria workers to Helen Fraed, the financial aid director, knew me by name. I knew theirs. Through junior high and high school I had earned money as a cleaning lady. I knew that these so-called support jobs were really essential to everything that went on, and that the people who did them at JU were as dedicated to doing their jobs as I was to getting an education. They helped keep me grounded and would often remind me that I should not forget where I had come from.

On the other hand was Terry Evenson. A White self-made

millionaire, he lived halfway across the country. I'd never met him, though we often spoke by phone. I gave him updates about my academic progress and campus activities. I sent him copies of my grades and news clippings featuring me. He sent me newsletters from his business.

He was generous always, ready to cover as much of my tuition as I needed, though I still did my best to win scholarships, find grants, and earn money part-time. He followed my activities and dispensed advice (a lifelong habit), worrying that maybe I was spreading myself too thin with my RA (Resident Assistant) responsibilities, my jobs, singing in a choir, the Black Students Association, volunteer work, and, oh, yeah, classes. He wasn't just doing this because he was some White man who felt guilty. He cared.

Still, after four years, I harbored some suspicions. My friends teased me that Mr. Evenson (as I still called him) was part of a conspiracy. The Man was educating young Black people whom he'd later use in a fiendish plot. If they didn't go along, they'd be murdered.

"Oh, that's nice," I snapped. "Why can't you believe that there are genuinely good people in the world?" A few years later, though, when Terry (as he'd become) invited me and a group of friends to his lake home in Minnesota, I remembered my friends' jokes and wondered if this was where the conspiracy would be exposed.

In between "Mr. Evenson" and "Terry," though, I was almost derailed by another perceived conspiracy. When the time rolled around for me to graduate, I was hurt because none of my Delaware family would be attending. I wasn't close with them again yet, but I was the only family member to have gone this far. It was an important event.

They all had reasons for not coming. Either they couldn't

afford it or they couldn't get off work. But, to my mind, they'd had four years to save up and prepare for this day, and that's what I told them when I told them off.

I knew what I was going to do. I decided to skip the graduation ceremonies. The ceremony wasn't for me; it was for other people who cared, and I didn't have any.

Sally Myers heard about this and practically ordered me to show up. She said that I had worked too hard to miss out. I told her I had other memories to hold, memories of late-night study sessions; of Phoebe, the mentally retarded woman who worked in the cafeteria and knew every student by name; of that special place in the library that was all mine; and of the advanced evolution exam that had almost killed me. I didn't need another memory to add to these: of a hot day and hundreds of caps and gowns, of a speech that no doubt would have nothing to do with me, spoken by someone who had no real sense of what I'd been through to get from there to here.

Sally told me to get over it. She also told me that in addition to Mr. Evenson, I would have other guests: The entire cleaning staff had requested to attend so they could see "their girl" go across the stage. I decided to attend and was glad that I did.

JU gives its President's Cup each year to one student who represents scholastic achievement and leadership. I sat in the audience listening to the description of the winner's accomplishments, trying to figure out what other RA had been in the choir, the theater arts group, and was from Wilmington, Delaware. Wow, I thought. I've been here for four years and I've never met this person.

Finally, when my friends started pointing at me and cheering, I realized that I was about to be called. That it was me.

My first day at JU flashed back into my mind. I was not

only on this list of graduates, I was at the top of that list. I cried. I still do when I think about it.

Dizzy with emotion, I walked up to the podium to receive the award from Dr. Linus Pauling, winner of the Nobel Prize in chemistry and the Nobel Peace Prize. As he gave me the cup, he whispered in my ear, "Young lady, soon you're going to be even greater than this."

I looked out over the crowd. Everyone was standing and cheering for me. I saw the cleaning staff, some in uniform, standing in a group with tears in their eyes. Some of them had not even graduated from high school, so they recognized the importance of an education. Their pride made me proud.

My best friend Rhonda's father, Ring Williams, ran up to the podium to help me down the steps. Though I never knew what it was like to have a father, at that moment I felt I did.

I'd seen pictures of Mr. Evenson in the newsletters he'd sent. I tried to find his face in the crowd but couldn't. (You know, all audiences look the same.) But after the ceremony he broke through the group of well-wishers and introduced himself. He apologized for not having seen the ceremony.

"What do you mean?" I asked.

He explained that a few days before coming to Jacksonville he'd had surgery to repair an old nose injury that was making it difficult for him to breathe. He'd already nearly choked to death when packing gauze from the surgery had dislodged and gotten stuck in his windpipe. This morning a severe nosebleed had kept him from being on time.

I looked at him and said, "And you still came?"

He told me that he wouldn't have missed this day for the world. We hugged and he told me how proud he was.

That night he took me and Rhonda to our first four-star restaurant. We were nervous about being in such a fancy place. When the busboy came by between courses to clean the table, Rhonda thought the small ribboned brush was a present. "Where's mine?" she asked.

We laugh about it now, but we were mortified then. Terry told us it was okay; he'd made bigger mistakes himself. I thought about the dinners Chris had taken us out to and where her example had led me.

Mr. Evenson presented me with a graduation present of $500—and the promise of his support for graduate school. He'd only met Rhonda that day, but he turned to her and told her that he'd support her, too. We thanked him over and over, but finally, near the end of the meal, I gathered my nerve to ask the question I had been waiting four years to ask.

"Okay," I started, trying not to sound nervous. "Why are you helping me? I mean, really, what do *you* want in return?"

Instead of the Charles Manson laugh my friends had told me I'd hear, Mr. Evenson smiled comfortably and said, "Well, first of all, I want you to get a good education, and then a good career, one that you will enjoy. And then I want you to pay me back. I'll put the money into a fund that will do the same for others. When you've paid me back and you're comfortable in life, I hope you'll think about doing the same thing for somebody else."

"That's it?" I asked him a little too suspiciously.

"That's a lot."

I knew then that I had found an angel and a friend.

So I'm In. How Do I Get Out?

By the time I had decided to go to graduate school, I was no longer waiting for signs. I didn't have to. I knew what I

needed and went after it. Kent State was one of several graduate schools I had applied to. I selected Kent because it met two
important criteria: It sent me my first acceptance, and its aid
package was generous.

I flirted with the idea of attending Oklahoma State, whose
acceptance arrived a little later with similar financial aid. I
was intrigued by the possibility of exploring my Cherokee
roots in Oklahoma. But when I called them, the person I
spoke to informed me that they were happy to be getting a Black
person.

A Black person, I thought. I had always been proud of
being Black, but I was also proud of the accomplishments I
had worked for. I didn't like the sound of the conversation and
went back to my original plan—I decided on Kent State.

It was a good choice, but in many ways, I felt completely
unprepared for it.

One of my first classes was in sociological theory. Dr. Paul Sites
was the professor, and when he entered the room he went to the
blackboard and started our first lesson in the middle of a sen-
tence. It was as if he were simply picking up a lecture right where
he'd left off the day before. I was thinking that I had missed a
week of classes but, in fact, this was the beginning.

My fellow grad students sat there and nodded their heads,
taking notes as if they, too, spoke this new, foreign language. I
left class thinking, What have I gotten into? I felt out of place
and could hear the muppets singing, "One of these things is
not like the other."

I rushed to the library for a refresher course. That term I
read as many sociological theory books as I could fit into my
schedule. I asked tons of questions of Dr. Sites in class and visited him and all of my other professors during office hours.
Who cared if I looked like I was behind? I had to catch up.

When exam time rolled around, I was suddenly the most popular student in class. My comfortable classmates all wanted to study with me. I asked why, since they obviously knew so much more than I did. *Au contraire*. Their nods had been an act to cover up the fact that they knew nothing. Since I had at least been able to ask questions about the material, that meant I must have understood it. "One of these things is not the same. . . ."

Before you get into a Ph.D. program, no one ever tells you what it's like. It's as if those who made it through are sworn to a vow of secrecy, promising never to reveal the initiation rites of the Grand High Order of the Ph.D.

Someone once told me that the most difficult thing about getting a Ph.D. is getting into the program. Ha! The hard part isn't getting in, it's getting out. There's a reason why there aren't that many Ph.D.s. The course work alone takes about four years to complete. You take four or five courses a semester. You don't have any exams, only research projects on which you receive very little direction. You can be doing fine or you can be doing terribly—only you know for sure. Anything less than a B at the graduate level is a failing grade.

Then there is the comprehensive exam. "Comps" cover *all* the material you are supposed to know in your chosen field of study. To prepare for them, you have to review everything you ever learned. When you're preparing for them, nothing else matters and everything gets twisted around so that it fits within the confines of what you're reviewing.

I was walking to the library one day when I passed a homeless man muttering to himself. Ah, I said to myself. Comps. I wonder what department he's in.

I took my comps in stratification, the distribution of wealth, power, and prestige in society. My emphasis was in several subareas: family, race, aging, gender, statistical research, and theory. The fact that my examination committee was composed of about twice as many professors as usual was a clue that I was being a little more ambitious than I needed to be, particularly since you can only pass by the unanimous decision of the committee. The more professors, the more likely it is that a lone dissenter can hold you up and make you repeat the entire process.

The exam had only six questions. Only? Each answer was about twenty-five pages long. At the end of the exam I went outside and threw up. But I passed the first time around.

Finding a Few Cheerleaders

At Kent, as at JU, I found strength and support that was instrumental in keeping me moving.

My academic adviser was Dr. Mullins; I was also her research assistant. She had a reputation as a difficult woman. People stopped me in the hallways to prepare me for meeting her. They said things like, "I hear you'll be doing research with The Bitch."

"Oh, she can't be that bad," I responded. To which they replied, "You'll see."

And I did. Dr. Mullins was nothing like they said, yet like nothing I'd expected on my own. She was tough. But she was also incredibly bright and hardworking.

Dr. Mullins was a fantastic professor who constantly challenged the intellect of her students. To some, however, she was too much. She said whatever was on her mind and she never watered it down. Once, when I couldn't figure out a problem, she said, "Oh, you're just ignorant." She meant it literally, though: that I was lacking information about a certain fact. Information I could acquire. But if I chose not to, I would be the other kind of ignorant—I'd be stupid.

When Dr. Mullins liked you, you had a friend for life. Luckily, she liked me. She pushed me through that master's program, and she worked hard to keep my Ph.D. committee focused on the real issues when they were debating my writing style.

If Dr. Mullins was ahead of me, showing me where I could go, another woman was alongside me, helping me keep up the pace.

My second day in graduate school, I met Bernita Berry.

Bernita Berry. I didn't have to be hit across the head.

She was the other Black woman in the sociology Ph.D. program. We believe that we were both accepted because they thought we were the same person. In some ways we were—we were Black women at Kent.

This was not a coincidence. God knew we'd both need help.

Bernita and I had a lot in common. I wondered why we had so many relatives with the same name. When she told me that she had fourteen brothers and sisters, I figured that based on the laws of probability there was bound to be some overlap.

Bernita's parents own a farm in a small town in Georgia where half the town (the Black half) is related to her. She'd crack me up with stories about folks from Ludowici. She had a cousin who wore two toupees; the church piano player couldn't play the piano; and a visiting minister made up words: "We're glad you all *congrelated* here today to give thanks and praise to our *magilestic* Lord and Savior."

Bernita had worked her way through college in every job imaginable, from cocktail waitress to factory worker. When she told me she was leaving grad school because she couldn't afford it, I asked her to move in with me to cut both our expenses.

Our mutual cooking talents were a deadly combination. We

each packed on about fifty pounds. When we called the local ice cream parlor to arrange for a delivery, they'd say, "Oh, hi. This is the Berrys, right?" When a place that delivers food knows you by voice, you know it's time to cut back. Hearing ourselves pant as we watched TV was another sign. I headed back to working out and Bernita joined me.

The Color Thing

Working with Dr. Mullins, I had helped interpret research that showed that elite Black women came overwhelmingly from mothers who had a high level of education. I was daring to think that I could be an "elite Black woman," but this was discouraging news. There was no high-level education in my background.

The research showed that other factors also influenced the success of Black people. Skin color was one of them. I knew this for a fact and had experienced it firsthand. I remembered a jump-rope rhyme from my childhood that went like this:

> *If you're light*
> *You're all right,*
> *Brown, stick around*
> *But if you Black*
> *Get way back.*

As an adult I'd hear Black people discussing how someone was "too Black" for them. They'd say things that would never have been tolerated from Whites. I needed to understand this in the hopes of being more prepared to educate Blacks in the areas of self-esteem and, consequently, community development. There is a great deal of division in the Black community, and unfortunately, much of it is along the color line. I chose to deal with it.

To say that my professors didn't understand the phenomenon is putting things mildly. Many could barely understand their own prejudices let alone how a Black person could discriminate against another Black person because of skin color. Few Whites even bother to distinguish color differences among Blacks. I had to educate my committee about a problem they didn't even know existed so that they could guide my research. Talk about twisted.

My work was not only laborious, it was downright upsetting. I did questionnaire interviews with Black teenagers to assess their attitudes concerning skin color. I asked them what color they thought they were, if they would change it, and if so, whether they would go lighter or darker. I also asked if they had experienced color discrimination, and if so, how often and from whom.

I took samples from a Black environment (the U.S. Virgin Islands) and predominantly White environments (Ravenna and Kent, Ohio). The results were exactly what I expected but didn't want to be right. The teenagers I'd interviewed in both sample groups had been taught that features closer to White were "better." They'd accepted this teaching, and it was constantly reinforced by the music videos they watched, the magazines they read, and their families and friends. To say that this depressed me is an understatement.

It was hard organizing and presenting material that demonstrated something that was so horrible to me, but I knew that these issues had to be acknowledged so that they could be confronted. It was painstaking work, and for my oral defense of the dissertation, I had to be ready to verbally support everything I had written, every concept, hypothesis, conclusion, and citation.

Once again, some of my strongest support came from people outside the academic community.

After much searching, I had found a church home in a small Black Methodist congregation. These were wonderful, kind, extraordinary people who led ordinary lives. Most of them were working-class people. Although they did not have any experience with the Ph.D. process, they understood that I needed family around me. They provided it, along with hot meals on Sunday and periodic calls throughout the week to see if Bernita and I were all right.

My dissertation defense rolled around, and while it was one of the most difficult days of my life, it was one of the most memorable and amazing. I was well prepared, but I also had a rooting section.

Friends and fellow students often sit in on dissertation defenses to provide quiet moral support, nodding and flashing an occasional smile.

My defense was more like a revival. The members of my church attended in full force. Whenever I answered a question or made a point, there was a chorus of "mmmmhm" and "Amen" and "Talk about it, sister."

The committee members were completely outnumbered and outspirited. "Tell it—you know what you're talkin' about." (What is she talkin' about?)

Years later I discussed this with my friend Debra, who is Black and had also gotten a Ph.D. Debra was Catholic, and to my surprise all of the nuns from her church attended her defense, in full habit. Different religion, but the effect was exactly the same. No one had any more power than those praying sisters.

Of course, I passed. I don't remember any of the questions or objections. I was asked to rewrite a small section and that was it. I was done. I was Dr. Berry.

Free at Last

That classroom in Kent, Ohio, was a long way from the downtown bus in Wilmington where I'd tried to scare the White folks with the vision of a little Black girl who could read. I wonder if any of the people who had stood by me and cheered me on in my childhood years ever imagined exactly where my path would lead.

It could have taken me to so many other places. Into the traps that caught my sister Portia, into the arms of someone who didn't love me, or into stagnation.

Instead, thanks to determination and support, my path has taken me to places of excitement, possibility, and happiness.

I'll never tell anybody that education, formal or informal, is a miracle cure. Too often, you gain understanding but the people around you don't, and you feel like you're speaking a language that nobody understands. I worked at educating myself so I'd be as good as White people, but nobody bothered to tell the White folks. Nor did they bother to educate themselves about me.

So I've learned that education has nothing to do with trying to be better than anyone else. It has everything to do with being better than the self you were before. Once that happens, you're free to recognize old traps that have caught you and to see new paths you and everybody around you have overlooked.

My calling in life is to be happy and to pass that happiness on to others. It is to inform, educate, and entertain all at once. I've been able to realize that calling in many different careers and activities. I know that as long as I'm happy and passing that happiness along, I'm doing what I'm supposed to do.

CHAPTER SIX

Education: Giving It Back

A mind is a terrible thing to waste. But if you waste my time, I'll waste you.

—*Opening remarks to Sociology 101*

*W*e live in a world that places more value on formal education than on informal. We assume that a person with degrees is somehow better, smarter, and more deserving than a person who doesn't have them.

I've known people who haven't gotten beyond the eighth grade and are as smart as someone with three Ph.D.s. These are the kind of folks who amaze me. I want to be around them as much as possible, to learn what they've learned, and to hear how they've learned it.

Unfortunately, this society rarely places a value on their type of acquired knowledge. At work they train people who will become their bosses, and they keep the company going. Their employers praise their wisdom while denying them the salary they deserve. These commonsense people justifiably complain and yearn for more. They realize the inequity and complain amongst themselves but rarely do anything more to change their circumstances.

On the other hand, there are those who are loaded with degrees but lack common sense. Their occupations and salaries reflect their years of education and book smarts. They are rewarded with all the comforts that money can buy. But many of these degreed people are uncomfortable with themselves. They don't know who they are or what their purpose is in life. In an attempt to find acceptance, they move around in circles of people who are similar to them in outlook. They are not in touch with the real world, telling themselves that they don't need to be, since they are better than others anyway.

One type of learning is not superior to the other. They are simply complementary. Both are necessary. And once you possess them, you have to pass them on.

In graduate school I helped pay my way by teaching undergrad courses. It was there that I learned that educating others is a responsibility, a task, and sometimes a headache. It can also be a good time.

I was fired up by the learning process. I knew what it had done for me, and I wanted to share that. It was exciting to find good, eager students, but even more exciting to find the struggling, reluctant students and show them how to open the door.

When I am fabulously wealthy, I want to build condominiums everywhere for teachers and social workers, the people who improve society every day and mostly get stepped on for their efforts. I know why they put up with it, though; when you're excited about the power of learning, you want to share it, and in exchange you're ready to accept some intangible rewards in lieu of cash.

Pillars of the Community

I can remember a time when, even if they weren't getting huge salaries, teachers were gods. At least they were in our part of Wilmington. On Monday mornings we'd whisper about how one of our classmates had sighted a teacher in a grocery store buying something as common as toilet paper. We'd gasp in horror and disbelief.

Strangely, maybe sadly, this kind of reaction has been transferred to celebrities. I'd love to see people asking a teacher for an autograph or to appear at some mall. There would be these huge crowds of screaming fans, all anticipating the arrival of that person who has the power to shape young minds.

In the good old days, back when I had to walk twelve miles in the snow, uphill both ways, to get to school, teachers were given the same respect as doctors. If they diagnosed possible trouble at home, they'd visit that home in person, storming in as if they were the F Troop or Jesus Christ, asking all kinds of probing questions. Our parents wouldn't even talk back to them because these people had been their teachers, too. (I had a perfect attendance record and was an eager learner, so we never received one of those visits.)

If you missed a few days of school, you could expect a teacher on your doorstep to find out why. If you thought it was okay to miss your homework, you could expect a paddle on your bottom to show you why not. My teachers were strict, but they were a ray of hope; they held the key to a better life. They were beauty personified and intelligence glorified.

I attended separate and very unequal secondary schools, and I was fortunate to do so. Although my schools lacked physical resources, the teachers made up for it with dedication, creativity, and innovation. The people in power planned that we should have inferior educations. What they didn't know was that mine was far better than anything they could have expected for their own children.

Lacking up-to-date textbooks, our teachers incorporated news items into the lessons they taught. We learned from the race riots and the Vietnam War. When our teachers couldn't dip into their own pockets to buy special equipment, they brought in special speakers, who would speak from experience about the issue or place we were studying. Some of these speakers helped us to understand the dangers of drugs, and then they had us turn around and teach this lesson to the kids a grade below us.

Our teachers knew we were poor and they did all that they could to keep that poverty from sapping our attention and drive. Many of my elementary school teachers kept a brown bag of used clothes by their desk. If a child had an accident or was looking even worse off than the others, they'd reach into that bag. They made sure that every child who needed it was present for the free breakfast and lunch programs.

Now hold on a second, 'cause Sister Berry has to preach: Those free breakfasts no longer exist, and when I hear politicians propose that we do away with free lunches, I want to take away theirs—along with their haircuts, limousines, cellular phones, fax machines, and free plane rides. Who are the idiots who cheer such politicians on, acting as if they were winning a war against the system's most corrupt enemy? That *enemy* is a young child who might not otherwise get a decent meal. Do they know this? Do they care?

Our teachers sure did: They worked as hard as they could to instill values in us, values that didn't just hold our community together, but values that I know kept all Wilmington from blowing apart.

In April of 1968 I was in Mrs. Carnie's second-grade class. She was the jolliest teacher, and when she came into class one day with the saddest face I'd ever seen, I knew something was terribly wrong. She was carrying a radio, and she plugged it in at the front of the room and turned to us.

"Class, I have something very sad to tell you," she said. "The Reverend Dr. Martin Luther King Jr. has been killed."

Then she started to cry. We all cried. Mrs. Carnie turned on the radio, and even the announcer was crying. We kept weeping as we listened to the recordings of Dr. King's speeches that were being played.

Mrs. Carnie turned off the radio and told us that we could still hear Dr. King's voice and that we would always feel his presence. She told us that the man who had killed Dr. King was full of hate. *She also told us that just because he was White didn't mean that we should hate all White people.*

Violence silenced Dr. King's voice, but something very different diluted the message and example of the Mrs. Carnies of our community.

It was busing.

I graduated from the last all-Black class in Wilmington, Delaware. After that the entire school system was desegregated. At that time I thought desegregation would be a good thing. Whenever we'd go sing at White schools or participate in a scholarship bowl, I'd marvel at the condition of the buildings. They had all kinds of equipment and teaching tools we never saw.

I'd believed that desegregation was the only way to provide Black students with the same opportunities as White students, because even I had unwittingly absorbed many of the maxims of my racist society. A part of me really believed that a "White" education was superior. I wanted that superiority to rub off on me and the other Black children of Wilmington.

I was also reacting to those people who'd appear on the evening news saying things like, "I'm not a racist—some of my best friends are Black. I just don't want my child to have to go to school in those people's neighborhoods. It's too dangerous." I figured that if I were antibusing, I'd be on the side of these bigots. I wanted to help solve the race problem and make the world a better place.

But most of my Black teachers were against busing.

I didn't understand why then, but now I know they were against losing the ability to shape the minds of their students and their communities. The writer, anthropologist, and voodoo priestess Zora Neale Hurston was also against desegregation. She was raised in an all-Black community and was against the idea of destroying its flavor.

When the schools of Wilmington were desegregated, many of those in the Black communities were closed. The teachers were sent to work miles away from where they lived. Some had to move, which meant that the neighborhoods lost them as resources and models. The very people most concerned with educating and uplifting Black students were taken away from them. It's clear to me that the harm to the community and our young people that resulted continues today.

Them That Can Teach

My first years of graduate school were spent as a research assistant. I spent huge amounts of time in the library and computer lab and very little with people. I began to question my commitment to helping people, the very force that had propelled me into sociology in the first place. Teaching seemed the logical and exciting alternative.

So I switched to a teaching assistantship. After a year working with a professor, I spent the next three on my own, trying to pass along my passion to undergrads.

My first solo assignment was introductory sociology. The

class had only thirty-five students, which was small on a campus of twenty-something thousand. I thought the intimacy was wonderful; the sociology department thought it was the best way to see how I did while minimizing any possible damage to those tender young minds.

I took cues from my elementary school teachers, who'd incorporated current events into our assignments, and from Drs. Mullins and Sites, who'd searched for social relevance as they taught theory. Since human behavior is both interesting and bizarre, I added the element of "funny."

My classes grew bigger and bigger and they were always packed. It wasn't just my eager students either; people would hear laughter and applause coming from my lecture halls and would wander in. They'd stand in the back until I'd yell for them to "come on down!"

I gave assignments that required the students to do outside research. When I taught the section on race relations, my idealistic young charges didn't want to believe they lived in a racist society.

So I paired the class up by race and gender: Black men with White women and White men with Black women. Since we were a trifle short of Black folks, I assigned the leftover White students to act as observers of these pairs. The pairs were sent out into the real world and told to act like couples.

I sent one set of students to a jewelry store, where they were to act as if they were looking for an engagement ring. They refused to do it! "That's okay," I told them. "I've got the grade book."

Other students went arm in arm to the cafeteria. They were upset when their friends—Black and White—stopped speaking to them. Even after they explained the assignment, they were still treated as outcasts.

"Great," I told them. "You're learning about racism, and tomorrow you get to experience homophobia. Bill, you take Bob." Hah!

My success with introductory sociology put me in line for teaching statistics as well. I was worried that this dry material wouldn't lend itself to the same fun approach of my other classes, but it did.

On Halloween we all went out as a normal bell-shaped curve. Of course, I was the mean.

Too Funny? Too Smart?

Teaching was not only fun for me, but I made sure that the students had fun as well. Whenever I was evaluated, I was told that I was a gifted teacher and that, with one exception, I was almost perfect: I was "too funny."

One professor told me that if I continued to be too funny, my students might miss the entire point of the lecture. I disagreed, but since I was trained as a social scientist, I decided to test my hypothesis.

I went through an entire lecture without telling any jokes or stories. After class I was mobbed by students. They wanted to know if I was okay, if my puppy had died. Class had been so boring, and one student said we hadn't covered as much material as we usually did. She was right.

Humor was a quick way to help my students understand the material. It made the theory accessible, understandable, and easier to remember. It brought the material to life, and if it did that, I knew I was doing what I wanted to do as a teacher. I went back to humor.

I faced criticism from another quarter, this one not even

human. The school's computer was used to grade exams. Students filled in their multiple-choice, true-false answers on a sheet that the computer scanned. Out popped scores and an analysis of the results.

Many of my students got A's on their exams. To me, this was a sign that I had done a good job teaching and that my students had done a good job learning. The computer disagreed. I got a notice from the computer that because so many of my students had gotten A's, there was only one explanation. The test was too easy.

There's a very debatable theory of intelligence that says a small percentage of people are extremely bright and a small percentage of people are extremely dumb. Everyone else is in the middle. This is represented by the dreaded bell curve and looks something like this:

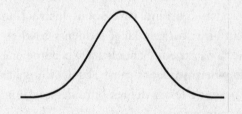

The whole thing is more complicated than this, but it's all said in statistical jargon that no one, not even most people who advocate the theory, understands. I do not advocate this theory; I have lots of problems with this theory.

Nothing about the bell curve examines or accounts for the role of the instructor. There's a huge variable that is simply not factored in.

If the bell-curve theory were true, then my students were (1) not normal and (2) not randomly assigned to my class.

But rather than take on the academic establishment, I

switched tactics. I got rid of multiple-choice tests and began giving essay exams. These essays took much longer for me to grade, but they were a better indicator of whether my students understood the material.

The same percentage of students got an A, but I discovered a terrible fact: Many of my students, who were juniors and seniors, had never written an essay for an exam. They got the tests and nearly passed out. "What do you mean, 'apply the theory'? I don't understand," they said in a panic. After several practice sessions most of them got the hang of it. A few took a bit longer, but I stayed with them and they eventually caught on.

Wildflowers Don't Need to Be Destroyed

Too often today, teaching isn't about instruction. It's about weeding out. Institutions label students so their bosses can know what to pay them. Schools have become one-stop learning centers where students must absorb things the first time around or accept a lesser degree of understanding. This is not the point of education.

When I was learning how to tie my shoelaces, my mom and Chris didn't stop after one try and send me out the door, tripping over my own feet with a big ol' F on my forehead. They simply said, "Try again." Okay, they yelled it. But the point is, I got another chance.

In my high school there was a boy who was a slow learner. Our teachers didn't abandon him; they worked with him to find out what he was good at, what he enjoyed. They discovered that he loved auto shop and they encouraged him at it. Today he is an independent businessman with his own auto-detailing shop, one of Wilmington's most successful. Those teachers did right by him.

Karen Denton still teaches in the public school system, and through the years we have remained good friends. Now, she says, the concern that we got in high school hardly exists. Students who act out for attention or love or because of vulnerability (sound like anyone you've read about lately?) are often packed away in learning-disabled classes. They may be bright, or even gifted, but because they have the wrong attitude, the wrong family, or the "wrong color," few of the teachers do anything to find out why the students behave as they do.

Instead, teachers are encouraged to report discipline problems so these students can be permanently expelled from school. This is a travesty. What kind of society punishes children by refusing to educate them?

In my own classes, I told my students that if they didn't get an A the first time around, they could continue to take other variations of my exams until they did. There was no possibility of memorization; study was required. Some students were grateful for this, but others, usually those who would get an A on the first attempt, felt my policy was unfair.

"Will their A count the same as mine?" they asked. When I said that it would, they said they felt cheated out of the accomplishment of getting the A on the first try. When I reminded them that this meant they would have more leisure time while other students had to study harder, they'd say, "Oh, okay."

I marveled at how effectively the system had socialized students to feel that education was a game that they had to win instead of a tool that everyone had the right to acquire.

Many of my students would tell me that they worked harder in my class than any other, but that they enjoyed the challenge. Some told me that they could no longer be satisfied with a C in any class and would study harder now, not only for an A but for the satisfaction of a better grasp of the material.

That was the kind of change I had hoped to make in the world.

I wanted my students to learn. I employed every technique I could think of, and if they failed, I tried others.

I had one student who was alert in class and studied hard. He'd come by for office hours and we'd get into theoretical discussions. But he consistently failed the exams. When I saw his look of disappointment as I returned his exams to him, I felt I'd failed, too.

I decided to administer an oral exam to this student. He continued to have a difficult time explaining the sociological theories, so I took another approach. He was a football player (stop stereotyping) and was well versed in the language of sport. I knew a little, so I asked him to apply the various sociological theories to some aspect of football.

He was brilliant. Not only could he apply the information, *he was capable of teaching it to me from his perspective*. I told him that this was good, but for the sake of his other classes he'd have to learn the academic language and the standard test-taking technique. Once he had found the avenue to understanding and was convinced that he was not a dunce, he was able to do this and did well in all his classes. He became a more dedicated student and is now a high school teacher.

I'm happy to know that the talk show and my lectures around the country have had the same impact. I recently met a college student who told me that she'd heard me speak the previous year and that I had changed her life. Prior to hearing me, she'd been flunking out in a major she didn't even like.

I had encouraged the audience to find their purpose, the one that made them happy. She did. She switched majors and took on a larger class load, but she was now on the dean's list and enjoying every moment of it.

A Burden We All Bear

My experience with these students is what I was thinking about when I called this chapter "Education: Giving It Back." Because I believe so strongly in the power and value of education, I believe I have an obligation to turn other people on to its value. I may have given up the day-to-day routine of leading undergraduate courses, but that sense of obligation has stayed with me on stage and screen.

I'm glad to say that I've often found the same spirit in other people. When I was researching colorism within the Black community, I helped conduct a forum on it at Kent State. Spike Lee came and showed *School Daze.* He took questions afterward. I cringed as I listened to university students ask questions like, "Why come the light-skinn-ded people are pretty and the dark ones are so damned ugly?"

Spike tried to point out that the dark sisters were gorgeous, but so many of the people in the audience couldn't see it. The problem is big, but Spike continues to take it on.

Bill Cosby and his wife, Camille, are constantly giving back. Once, after Camille had seen me perform, she told her husband that I was extremely talented. Mr. C. invited me to a taping of *The Cosby Show* and afterward to dinner. Then he took me aside privately for about an hour and told me how to be successful personally, financially, and emotionally. I was amazed that someone so busy would be so concerned with the path of another.

When I told my mother that I had had dinner with Bill Cosby, she said, "Someday you will."

You don't have to be a celebrity or a millionaire to give back. I'm often moved by the random acts of kindness of everyday people. A segment we had planned for *The Bertice Berry Show* fell through. My producer, Sol Feldman, and I decided that we didn't want to lose the production cost. That night we went out to find another story. It was one of the coldest nights of the year in Chicago; the wind off the lake was like a razor.

Joined by one of our security officers, Dwayne, and our cameraman, Aaron, we went in search of street prostitutes. We wanted to do a show that gave an accurate account of their lives. It was about 9 P.M. when we went out, and I know it was past 3 A.M. by the time I got home.

The women, men, and transvestites talked to me candidly about their lives on the streets. One said that she had been beaten up at least fifty times, raped eleven, and shot twice. All of the prostitutes we talked to were drug addicts. I'd imagined that they became prostitutes to support their drug habit. But they said it was the other way around. "Imagine doing ten to twenty-five blow jobs a night straight," one told me.

They were often mothers and always somebody's child. Their families knew what they were doing but didn't want to hear it.

We were heartbroken by what we heard. Aaron was teary-eyed. He gave his gloves to one of the prostitutes and refused to charge us overtime. "Your work is important," he said. When I got home that night to my two-story condo, I took a long, hot shower and cried.

The next day some of the prostitutes came to the studio to do the show. They were honest and compelling. The audience members, mostly middle-class White women, could feel their pain. At the end of the show the prostitutes received a standing ovation. The next day a group of audience members came back. They had collected $500 to give to a shelter for prostitutes who try to turn their lives around.

When people hear about my accomplishments, they're amazed that someone so young can have done so much and still be alive. It doesn't seem so strange to me. I'm following the most basic of all rules: What goes around comes around. The more I give back to others, the more opportunities come my way. The more doors I hold open, the more that are open for me.

CHAPTER SEVEN

Work:
The Other Four-Letter Word

People ask me what the transition is like, going from teaching to comedy.

I ask them, "What transition?"

I was often doing both at the same time. I had a comedy gig in Virginia, a dissertation chapter due the following morning in Ohio, and a class to teach. Instead of teaching my class how to reject the null hypothesis, I found myself doing stand-up:

"Buckwheat became a Muslim. His new name is Kareema Wheat."

I've been working for the last twenty-three years. I've taken a few breaks here and there from employment, never very long. I've put together a résumé that just about entitles me to run a small planet. I've had almost every kind of job I can think of—and a few I never want to think about again.

I'm fortunate that early on I learned the importance of doing my best at whatever job I had and to use the experience to take me to the next one.

My Life as a Cleaning Woman

When I was twelve, I tagged along with my friend Barbara Dorsey and her mom on one of Mrs. Dorsey's cleaning jobs. At the time, it was just a chance to earn some money helping out, but what I got out of that day was worth every penny I've earned since.

I marveled at how Mrs. Dorsey knew how to do everything. She moved like a ballerina, polishing silver and crystal, cleaning bathrooms and ovens. I badgered her with questions:

What's that little brush for? What do you use to clean mirrors? I thought you couldn't mix those cleansers.

Mrs. Dorsey took it all in stride and explained everything. She pointed out the proper way and the quick way of doing everything. The quick way, she said, should only be used occasionally, if you were really pressed. "It will get you by," she said, "but after a while the slacking off becomes noticeable."

There was no shame in domestic work when I saw Mrs. Dorsey do it. When the job was done, she had transformed the place. Everything had a new sparkle and shine. A marvelous feeling of pride came over me, and I knew that whatever work I did in life, it should give me that same feeling.

When I got *The Bertice Berry Show,* I knew I had to put the same dedication into my work there. From the beginning we pitched the show as an alternative to the other talk shows in the market. We had an intense screening process to interview all the prospective guests. Strange as it may seem, some people will lie and degrade themselves in order to get on television. We always caught them. Once a transvestite claimed to be pregnant. "Yeah, and Bertice is, too," a producer said before hanging up.

I was also determined that we weren't going to plant words in the mouths of our guests. This was at odds with the way things were done on at least *some* other shows; I knew this from staff members who'd been there. They had worked in the school of producing that said the guest should be attractive and a good talker, someone who told a story quickly and said it in standard English. I felt that if the story was compelling enough, people would prefer it to some packaged, glamorized version.

The best example of this was a show titled "Misdiagnosis

Ruined My Life." Our lead guest had a *very* leisurely Southern drawl and wore an old corduroy jacket. Plus, he was nervous.

Making this man the lead guest defied conventional talk-show wisdom. He wasn't going to get all fired up and angry, and he wasn't going to say bizarre and outrageous things. What he gave us was compassion.

When he told his story, he painted a picture of his home with a porch and hanging flowers. He talked of his mother, who had a knack for making things bloom and for taking care of the family. She had been diagnosed with cancer. Because her mother had died a lingering, painful death from cancer, she didn't want to endure the same.

She asked her son to bring her a gun. He didn't want to, but she pleaded with him. He gave in, and she killed herself.

An autopsy revealed that she never had cancer.

I wept; everyone wept. This man tactfully illustrated that people thought doctors were gods and havoc could result from blindly following them. I know there was no stronger way to make that point.

This same show revealed another standard to us, a principle I am proud to say we upheld against relentless pressure from executives.

We brought on a couple whose baby had become deformed because of a misdiagnosis. Her legs and arms hadn't grown properly, and she had no hands or feet. They wanted to bring their daughter onto the set with them.

Bonnie Kaplan, who was then our creative consultant and later the show's executive producer, said no. She pointed out that children can understand what is being said even earlier than we realize. She didn't want to give this little girl the impression that she had been *ruined*. I remembered all the times I was called a "no-good, worthless bitch," and I agreed.

I had better memories to guide me. We knew the proper way of doing our show and we didn't slack off.

Hallelujah, I'm Working

Thanks to the example Mrs. Dorsey set for me, I was soon able to get work of my own cleaning houses. There were many cleaning ladies in my church, and word of my skills spread. One of them took me under her wing and taught me more about the personal satisfaction of a job well done.

She was my Sunday school teacher, and her name was Sister Evangelist Lucille Treadway. She said that God wanted her to be called by that name, so that's what we called her. You couldn't shorten it; you had to say the whole thing: Sister Evangelist Lucille Treadway.

Sister Evangelist Lucille Treadway cleaned banks at night. She and I would work in these huge, empty places, glass walls all around us. It was kind of scary. People could see us inside, but we couldn't see out; we always had this feeling of being watched, possibly by burglars waiting to break in.

We kept the fear of the Dalton Boys away by singing songs of praise, belting out "You Don't Know Like I Know" and "My Soul Says Yes" in between the Sunday school lessons that Sister Evangelist Lucille Treadway gave me as we cleaned.

Our biggest scare didn't come from a modern-day Ma Barker, though.

One night, when we arrived at our first bank of the evening, I heard a noise in the basement. Sister Evangelist Lucille Treadway told me to go check it out. I wondered why she didn't go herself, but I was young and cocky, so I went, toting a mop and bucket down a dark stairway.

I got to the third step and suddenly the lights came on.

"Freeze!"

Two big White police officers were pointing their guns right at me. I froze.

"What are you doing here?" one of them shouted.

I was frightened, but I was even more angry. One more step and I could have been Little Dead Cleaning Lady. "What does it look like? I'm here to clean. Wanna help?"

"Don't get smart," the other one snarled. Obviously these guys had never heard of the good-cop/bad-cop routine. "What's your name?" he asked. I desperately wanted to say, "Pudden Tang. Ask me again and I'll tell you the same," but I didn't. It would have been wasted.

"Bertice."

"What's your last name, Beatrice?"

"Bertice," I corrected. "Bertice Berry."

The other officer told me that there had been an attempted robbery the night before and they had been sent to watch over things. No one had told them about Sister Evangelist Lucille Treadway and me. And nobody had thought to warn us about them either.

No one thought us important. What a crazy world we live in. We save our adoration and praise for doctors, but without cleaning people, even doctors would be sick.

Wilmington's finest may have taught me to be wary, but Sister Evangelist Lucille Treadway had taught me a more important lesson about giving thanks for the opportunity to work.

On Sundays, when it was time to pay tithes (10 percent of your earnings that go to the church, as taught in the Bible), the church youth would sit up straight, waiting for Sister Evangelist Lucille Treadway to go into her routine. She would go shouting and dancing up to the tithe box. "Hallelujah! Thank you, Jesus, thank you, Jesus. Hallelujah," she'd holler. The young people would muffle their laughter and try not to shake.

Before I'd started working with Sister Evangelist Lucille Treadway, I'd laughed, too. But once I saw what she really did, I knew why she shouted that way. She was blessed. She had work that she enjoyed, and with two sons to raise on her own, she welcomed every penny it brought her.

Not Where I'm Not Wanted

In my senior year of high school I gave up my cleaning work in order to concentrate on the Upward Bound program. I was getting quite accustomed to having a little money and I didn't want to give up my job. But Mr. Morris, the director of Upward Bound, pointed out that if college didn't work, I could always fall back on my cleaning. I got the point. I took with me the work ethic I had learned from those proud women with whom I'd cleaned house.

During the terms at JU, I had my work as an RA and in the campus post office. During breaks, I took any available job. I worked at fruit stands, did inventories in retail shops, and once, but only for one day, I worked as a waitress.

That one day gave me the utmost respect for people who serve food for a living. One time I served wine and snacks at an outdoor concert, and the customers were incredibly rude. They acted as if the Emancipation Proclamation had never been signed. I asked a friend who waitressed all the time how she managed, and she told me she just tried not to think too much about it.

I also learned an important adjunct to Berry's Rules of Relationships. There is a positive correlation between how well you treat your server and how well you treat your date. If you're rude to your server, it follows that you'll be rude to your date. If you ignore the server, you'll ignore your date. But then the paradigm shifts: If you stiff your server, your date will stiff you.

This experience brought home to me how little some people value hard work and at the same time how they don't understand how important it is to people's self-esteem. They let unimportant issues distract them, such as what you look like and what they think they know about you.

One summer I was back in Delaware, and the Summer Youth Programs got me a placement at the Delaware Technical and Community College as a lab assistant. I had it in the back of my mind that instead of social work I might try to become a chemical engineer, so this was a wonderful opportunity.

I arrived early for the interview, which was supposed to be nothing but a formality. I was happy to be greeted by a Black receptionist.

She looked me over and told me that I wouldn't do. I asked why and she pointed to my hair, which was braided in cornrows. I'd made sure they were neat for this day, so I wondered what she was talking about. She told me that braids were not "professional" and should not be worn to work. She said she expected someone "better," since my application said I was in college.

I was hurt that this Black woman was rejecting me because of my "Blackness," but I did not protest. I thanked her and left.

Initially I thought maybe she'd had a point. She was Black and she was working, so maybe she knew the proper way for Black women to go to work. Maybe she had even written a book about it. (That or maybe a carpentry manual on the construction of back doors.)

At the job center, my counselor was furious. She was ready to call this woman up and give her a piece of her mind. She said my hair was fine and my suitability for the job was hardly this woman's decision. I told her that I didn't want to work someplace where I wasn't wanted.

When I was battling my "favorite" executive about my hair and everything else on *The Bertice Berry Show,* I remembered this experience. I was determined that never again would my hair or anything else about the way I looked be used as a tool to make me into something I am not.

Sure, I work for the money; I've got three growing children to feed. But I'm also fortunate enough to be able to choose the work I do: I also work for happiness. There is no way that I will accept a situation where I have to tone down who I am to make somebody else happy.

I know that this is not a choice everyone can make, though I dream of a world that recognizes every job as valuable. I dream of a world where a janitor is as respected as a doctor, where a teacher has the prestige of an orthodontist. It's a long way off, but at one time, so was my right to vote.

R·E·S·P·E·C·T

When I was turned down for the lab assistant's job, the counselor told me that since I was considering social work, I might be interested in a position at the food-stamp office. I was interested in work, period. I ran over as fast as I could.

The supervisor who met me was a White woman. She said she was happy to be getting a college student and that she loved my hair. I got depressed that my hair had been rejected earlier by a Black woman but then accepted by someone

White. This self-hatred and acceptance of White standards over anything Black was something that drove my later research into colorism.

That summer I spent at the food-stamp office opened my eyes to how the government worked. It was stupid.

A food-stamp application could be processed overnight, but a person wouldn't receive the actual stamps until thirty days later. Only in cases of dire emergency were people able to get them any sooner.

I was able to identify some people who were trying to "get over" by getting more than their share of food stamps. Most often, children who were over eighteen would get stamps for themselves while they were living with parents who were claiming an allotment for them. I ran into these problems on occasion, but they were minor wastes compared to the bureaucratic cost.

The people I worked with in that office were efficient and fair, but not well paid. Administrative salaries, however, were enormous. Consultants and outside researchers received huge sums of money to observe things that the caseworkers already knew.

I learned how degrading it was to be poor and in need of government assistance. My mother had rarely asked for government help, so I wasn't fully aware of the treatment of poor people by government agencies. Most were ashamed to need the food stamps or ask for help at all.

In grocery stores I saw clerks abuse the recipients as they shyly handed the stamps over. "You know you can't use food stamps for cleanser," they'd loudly accuse so that everyone in the store heard them. "Separate the non-food-stamp items. Y'all come in here every month, but you never learn."

I'm embarrassed by the stupidity of those who think that all people who are receiving assistance are lazy and looking for a way to "get over." Having been poor, I know that this isn't the case. It's a lot easier to work at a job that gives you dignity and respect than it is to stand in line waiting for help.

Stand Up and Laugh

If I had a problem with being on the stand-up circuit, it was that in many ways it could erode people's self-respect. Comedians are some of the hardest-working people in the world, but they can also be the most catty. They tear each other down on everything from the originality of a joke to the clothes they wear.

"You're not wearing that out there?" one would say to another right before going on. They knew that all a comedienne has is her material and her confidence. You can pull off weak material with strong confidence. But even the best material can't be delivered unless you've got some kind of presence.

I also saw an incredible amount of destructive behavior. Many comics were constantly drinking and doing drugs. Many of the men had a different woman in their room every night, sometimes every few hours. This wasn't my thing and sometimes I felt as if I were Cousin Marilyn in *The Munsters*.

But there were and are some great people out there on the road. The women comics were always helpful, and I was glad to work with them on those rare occasions when two of us were on the same bill. Margaret Smith actually gave me a list of comics I should never stay in the same hotel with; some of them had actually been convicted of rape.

Diane Ford was so funny that we sometimes forgot we had to go onstage. She told terrific war stories of the holes that she'd played. I had some of my own. On the road, doing comedy in 250 different places each year, I sometimes had to work hard to remain thankful for the opportunity to be out there, as well as face some entirely unexpected risks. Aside from my ability to get lost, the worst thing about the road was staying in the "Comedy Condos." These place should have been called Roach Motels.

Local clubs had to pay for our accommodations and would put us into filthy dives that had usually been torn apart by the last group of comics to pass through. I carried my own sheets and cleanser and always had a spare shower curtain in my trunk.

My cousin Robin was traveling with me as my road manager once when we stopped in a teeny-weeny little town in the middle of nowhere. Except, as it turned out, it wasn't the middle of nowhere. It was a major transfer point on a drug route.

One of the first things that I did for myself after I started making real money at stand-up was buy a set of Halliburton luggage. I thought it was sleek and elegant, and in my innocence I didn't realize that *Miami Vice* had made them the suitcases of choice among sleazy drug runners.

Robin and I had walked into a room at the worst hotel I had ever been booked into, taken one look, and decided to do what ghosts say: Get out! The beds were sunken in the middle, and there was hair on the bar of soap. I should have known not to go into any motel room with a combination lock on the door.

We were taking our luggage back to the car to head out for someplace with higher standards when a man leaned over the balcony above us and said, "Manny wants to know what you're carrying."

Innocent little me. I didn't know what he meant. I shrugged my shoulders.

Some of my more informed friends later explained that exchange to me. The man on the balcony was asking, "Manny wants to know what you're holding." My shrug meant, "Lots of things, but I ain't selling to you, sucker."

"Manny's not gonna like this," the man growled. As he turned around to go back into the room behind him, the scales fell from my eyes and I noticed five or six other guys, none of whom had probably kissed their mother in years. I started hearing the music from *West Side Story*, you know that tune: "There's Gonna Be a Rumble."

I left tire marks in the parking lot.

Road life wasn't all bad. In fact, there were some great moments when other comics encouraged me, guys like Steve Harvey and A. J. Jamal. Richard Jeni, one of the funniest people alive, told me that I was very funny and that I had the biggest *cojones* (balls) of any man, woman, or alien.

When I was still juggling academia and stand-up, a friend of mine sent a tape of one of my performances to Sinbad. The tape had my home number on it, and Sinbad called and left me a message: "Hey, this is Sinbad. Girl, you got it going on. Keep on keeping on—but get your Ph.D."

I played that tape for everybody. Sinbad called three more times until he caught me at home. He encouraged me some more to work toward what he said would be a very successful career. This made me proud.

The best government program that could ever exist would be one that made people proud to do any job well.

Just Ten Minutes of Work?

Colleges are like prisons. Well, maybe not. At least in prison you know when you're going to get out.

The more I taught, the funnier I got. My students would

tell me I should be a comedienne, but I didn't give it any thought until Mike Veneman came along.

Mike was another graduate student who happened to be a comedian. (You ever notice that people only use "who happens to be . . ." when they're speaking of subdominants like women, Blacks, homosexuals, and comedians?) He told me that I should give stand-up a try.

Mike is hilarious. If he thought I was funny, then I must be. He was working toward his Ph.D. in sports sociology but later decided to quit since he realized he'd make more money and more observations as a stand-up than as a sociologist. When he first made his suggestion, though, I told him self-righteously that I was a serious scholar. He said, "You can't be; you're funny."

He harassed me until I finally gave in. He told me to prepare a ten-minute routine for an amateur competition. He said it was a breeze and that I could win fifty dollars. I thought I had gone deaf.

"Fifty dollars for ten minutes of work?" I asked.

"Well, something like that."

I soon figured out what he meant. It took me two weeks to prepare ten minutes of material that I thought was funny, and another two weeks to get it to where other people thought it was funny, too.

It was for this routine that I created my Tina Turner impersonation. I reasoned that since she was someone everybody knew, it would be easier for a White audience to like me being her.

I had bought my Tina wig the year before in a Korean wig shop. When I took it off the Styrofoam head, a tall transvestite hooker came running at me.

"Girl, I was gonna get that," she said in a voice huskier than mine.

I told her that I needed it for a Halloween party, and she told me that she needed it for work. "Mens love them some Tina Turner."

I felt kind of bad for her, but not that bad. I paid for the wig and dashed out of the store before she could run me down.

That first competition marked the night when I blanked on Tina's song and came up with the impromptu business that would be part of my act for years. Bernita had driven me and a bunch of friends. We'd gotten lost along the way, which made me the last competitor to arrive. What Mike hadn't told me was that the last to arrive would be the first to go on.

Now first is absolutely the worst spot in a lineup. The audience isn't warmed up yet and they sort of assume you're no good. Still, as you already know, I was a hit.

After I'd won the audience over with Tina, I put them at ease by telling jokes about racism.

I used pretty gutsy stuff for my first time out. I talked about the double standards for men and women. "Why do men always grab their crotch?" I asked.

"'Cause they want to point out that they're men! But women don't go around like this," I said, pushing my breasts together. "Hi, I'm Barbie."

I got a standing ovation and the crowd hadn't even had their second beer. I was proud.

My enthusiasm waned as I watched the other comics go up. They had skills. Their timing was almost perfect and so were their jokes. There were about eight of us, plus the club's bartender, who told jokes that he'd stolen from headliners. He performed last and closed with a sexist joke that went over big.

When it was time to announce the winner, we were all called back to the stage. The audience applauded for their favorite performers, and it was down to me and the bartender. The crowd cheered us equally and we were both declared winners.

I wondered how we could both be funny to the same audience. He told the kinds of jokes I hated, yet they liked us both. I decided just to be happy about the outcome and save the analysis for later.

Hittin' the Road

To actually get the fifty-dollar prize, I had to come back a week later and perform again. I immediately started writing new material, something that would impress the audience. I kept the Tina skit exactly as it was, though. People at the club started asking me questions about where I'd worked before and why they hadn't heard of me. No one believed that I had just started.

I liked the idea of using humor to teach and wanted to continue with that. I started watching other comics but soon realized that I had to have my own style. I often watched other comedians try to deliver "borrowed" material. To me it always stood out as someone else's. The audience wasn't always aware, but the comics would stand at the back of the room and point it out.

I began taking gigs at other clubs. I didn't know how to drive yet, so Bernita was always hauling me around. One of the club owners told me that he thought I was good enough to start working a bigger circuit; he put me in touch with Tom Sobol, a booking agent. Tom put together a month-long tour for me.

There were a couple of tricks to this. I was still teaching, and the tour ranged from Colorado to Florida, only about half the country. Naturally, I would have to drive. I had a car, didn't I?

Not only did I not have a car, I had never been behind the

wheel of one. I only had a few weeks to change all that. I had to get a driver's license, a car, and insurance. I was frantic.

Bernita, bless her, took me out driving and I almost gave her a heart attack. I failed the driver's test twice before my friend Tia came to my rescue with her sleek new Toyota and its power steering. I passed on my third and last try and ran out of the DMV like a nut.

We had to put the car I bought in Bernita's name, since no one would insure me, a new driver at my age with no credit record. The car was a used Honda with only 30,000 miles on it. Within the year I had taken it up to 180,000.

I was thanking God at every stoplight, but the work quickly started to wear on me. I was driving to gigs, doing my act, staying up all night to grade papers, then racing back to Kent to meet with my dissertation committee as soon as the sun was up.

My professors and advisers found out about my comedy career and weren't pleased. They felt that I wasn't taking my academic work seriously. I figured they had to be blind. I'd spent years working for a Ph.D., and nothing was going to keep me from getting it.

I was often pulled aside and admonished to give up my foolishness. They felt that as a Black woman I should recognize "my people's" need for more academicians and fewer "buffoons." I was offended, so I tried to offend them.

I started doing crazy things like wearing huge rabbit slippers in the hallways and telling jokes to anyone who'd listen. There was some *concern* for my mental state. Fortunately, I also got some encouragement. Dr. Mullins had actually seen me do my routine and urged me to continue. "Bert, you're going to have a bigger impact out there than they'll let you have in here."

Terry Evenson, my benefactor-turned-friend, had seen me perform and also encouraged me. I hadn't expected this; he was always cautioning me against doing too many things. I'd been afraid even to tell him I was doing stand-up, but when he gave his support, I felt I was on the right path.

With the support of these well-wishers and many others, I decided to complete my dissertation and embark on a full-scale comedy career. It was a big step, but I was used to taking big steps.

Hey, It's a Big Country

As I prepared to hit the comedy circuit, I had some misgivings. They weren't about what I was doing, but where I was doing it.

Comedy clubs can be skanky places. Too often some ugly drunks in the crowd think they're hilarious. Of course, they'd never get up onstage and try their stuff out for real, but that doesn't stop them from being a pain.

One of the first gigs that I had for pay was in a small town in Ohio at a bowling alley/comedy club/tavern. I was the opening act. I'd be paid twenty-five dollars a night. I thought that I had died and gone to pig heaven (wherever that is). I was soon in for a rude awakening. The Bowling Alley and Comedy Club was nothing like Hilarities, the club where I'd started. How could it have been? People were actually bowling there.

On my first night there, I was a huge hit, but not in the way I'd planned to be. I started out doing my regular routine, but the crowd wasn't paying attention. The few who were listening weren't laughing. Then out of nowhere, some guy started to heckle me.

I had plenty of comeback lines, most of them from my mother. "Oh, be quiet before I cut your ass too short to shit."

The crowd loved it. The louder he got, the sharper I became. People even stopped bowling to hear me.

When my ten minutes were up I felt as if I had spent a year in front of the mike. Folks were slapping me on the back and yelling stuff like, "Bring that colored girl back up."

I was a hit but I didn't like it. My reason for doing comedy had been to feel good about myself and to make others laugh while simultaneously informing them. My goal wasn't to tear folks down. God knows, we can all get that for free. But here I was ripping some drunk apart and feeling a sense of power because of it.

That night I prayed and told God that if comedy wasn't the place for me, then I would quit. I repeated my commitment to be positive and went to sleep.

The next night at the Bowling Alley and Comedy Club started out the same way. In an effort to help me out, the bartender started heckling me. But I didn't take the bait. I kept going with my routine. The whole thing was completely weird. People weren't paying any attention. I was doing my thing and the bartender was yelling insults. I forged on and eventually he stopped. When I got through, I figured that my fifteen minutes of fame were over. I walked down through the crowd and out to the bathroom.

On my way a woman stopped me. She said, "Honey, you're good. Just stick to your guns and you'll make it." Sometimes what's meant to be bad (oh, baby, by now you should know this) can turn out to be good.

One of the many gigs I took was with a cruise line. (Gosh, no, I didn't feel out of place. Why do you ask?) I had just finished my Ph.D. and was depressed. I was also having a hard time liking people. I figured that working with folks on a cruise ship would restore my faith in humanity. You can probably guess, I was buying shoes with swollen feet. I had fun, flying from ship to ship, doing stand-up for a few nights, then going on to the next ship. Yes, I had fun—in the morning, in the evening. Will somebody please tell Kathie Lee to stop singing that song.

Of course, since I only performed for a few hours each night, I had a lot of time at my disposal. Before becoming a flying-in act, as it's called, I'd had other duties and never a moment to spare, so I felt sorry for the other ship employees who worked for weeks without a break, and I was always glad to help out. Particularly at bingo.

I had a ball, and I packed the passengers in as I had packed my classrooms. I'd yell the numbers at them, and they thought I was cute: "Down the B-1, come on White people, B-1. Cover your stupid numbers." They would laugh as if I had called them beautiful.

It was amazing to see what I could get away with. In fact, it was all quite therapeutic. At least until one day when someone made me move my neck.

I was doing my usual routine and someone yelled, "Bingo."

"Okay," I shouted. "We've got a winner. Come on White lady, bring your card on down here so I can check it to tell if you cheated." She ran on down and was declared the winner.

The players cleared their cards and were starting a new game when some guy from way in the back yelled, "Hey, I've got bingo, too."

I wanted to say, "Too bad, pokey," but I never actually tried to be mean to these folks, so I said, "Well, sir, I'm sorry," imitating the stuffy accent of the English cruise staff, "but we've already cleared the boards."

The man became belligerent. He called me names he shouldn't have. I remained calm. The Black woman's burden. One of them.

Then came the Note.

The cruise director sent me a message from the back of the room, saying that he needed to instruct me on how to call bingo. I went to the back where he was counting the huge stacks of money I had just helped the cruise line make off the bingo players. I pointed out that I had been doing him a favor; bingo-calling was not part of my job description.

His attitude left something to be desired (a whole list of somethings: tact, graciousness, courtesy, respect). I told him that he could find himself a new bingo caller, and while he was at it, he could find a new comic. I was leaving.

"You cahn't," he said.

"And, pray tell, why shan't I?"

"Because we're at sea."

He had a point.

Not forever, Sherlock.

The staff cheered me.

It gave me great satisfaction to walk that plank. That was the only job I've ever walked out on in my life. I've always been dedicated to doing well whatever it is I'm paid to do.

I talked with Mike Veneman about my loss of enthusiasm toward comedy clubs and he suggested that I try performing at colleges. I didn't know any college agents in the United States, and neither did he, but he did know one in Canada.

The name Zoe Stotland will always conjure up memories of being lost in Canada.

Zoe is one of those women who became successful in a male-dominated field by being better than men at their own game. She must have booked me into every single Canadian college and university, every pub, club, and subway station. I didn't have any idea about the distances between these gigs, so I gladly took them all.

I worked two, sometimes three times a day, with little time off. I got lost in snowstorms more times than I want to remember. I never failed to show up for a gig, though. I still get a horrible feeling of claustrophobia when I'm lost in a car; I have to stop, get out, and catch my breath.

My friend Marty Putz, a hilarious prop comedian from Toronto, took to calling any roundabout tour "the Bertice Berry Tour." He'd call me in Medicine Hat to see if I was still alive and find out that I'd moved on to Moose Jaw.

I complained to Zoe about the work once. She told me to stop being a baby. Her tough attitude made me even more determined.

As much as I hated the travel, I loved playing those colleges. The audiences were sober and they loved my material. They'd come up afterward for lengthy discussions. Once they heard my credentials, professors would send entire classes to my performances for credit. I could be as intellectual as I wanted and as crazy as I felt. The combination was sweet.

When I first started in comedy, I met Robert Townsend at a club in San Diego. I was there with a bunch of friends, and we were all on the floor with laughter after his performance. His comedy was what I had lived. (I got a bit upset when he did a Black Shakespeare routine, though. I had only been doing stand-up for about a month. I had about fifteen minutes of material. Three of my minutes were based on the same Shakespeare premise. I would have said he stole his from me, but I knew better. His was brilliant and very polished—okay, he made me sick.)

The people at our table were the loudest in the place, and after his performance Townsend came over to thank us for getting it. I immediately started pumping him for information. I wanted to know how he was capable of getting away with material that was smart and funny but still militant. He told me that he wrote each joke to work on several layers, so that no matter where people were in their thinking, they could get something from it.

I learned to apply this technique to my own writing:

Periods are like airplane food. You don't want it, but if yours doesn't come, you go, "Where's mine?!"

I had once read a quote from television journalist Edward R. Murrow that had a great impact on my performances. He said to present the news as if it were being delivered to a professor at dinnertime, but to also assume that the professor's maid and her boyfriend, a truck driver, were listening from the kitchen.

Murrow was absolutely right. I've discovered an interesting thing about television: You don't always realize immediately who you're reaching, or how effectively you're doing it, or how much of an impact you're having. For example, even before *The Bertice Berry Show* was up and rolling, a brilliant director named Kevin Burns did a minidocumentary about my life. I'm still discovering how much of a reach it had.

One day when I was in the Atlanta airport, a woman who worked in security came running up to me for an autograph. I was tired and about to miss my flight, but I stopped anyway. She could have been an angel for all I knew.

She said her name was Tangelia.

"Could you spell that, please?" I said through clenched teeth.

I started thinking about the many autographs I'd signed for people with names like Shisquita, Malamesha, and Ondrika. (I once met a man whose name was V. I asked him what it stood for. He said, "I'm the fifth child.") I knew that their mothers were just trying to find roots for their children by naming them things that sounded less European. Without having any knowledge of their African heritage, they were trying on their own to come up with wonderful names like Na'im Akbar, Ntozake Shange, and Haki Madhubuti. But too often all they could come up with were names like Toyota.

Anyway, Tangelia said, "I need to tell you something."

"Okay," I sighed.

She told me that when she was a teenager, she had gotten pregnant and dropped out of school. She said that after the baby was born she was too embarrassed to go back. Then she had another child. Without a diploma or any job skills, she couldn't provide for her children. She started dealing drugs.

By now I'm thinking, I can catch a later flight.

Tangelia told me that one day she accidentally taped my show. It wasn't that she didn't like me, she just didn't like any talk shows. The show that she taped was the one about my life. She was moved by how I had made it against the odds, and how my life was proof that there were even some decent White folks in the world.

She said that learning about me had inspired her to get her life together. She'd gotten rid of her drug habit, gone back to school, earned her GED, and eventually gotten a job at the airport, where she still worked. She had even started college.

I thanked her for telling me and then held on to her as if I were the fan. I made it to the flight on time and cried all the way back to Chicago. By that time my show had been off the air for a year, but I realized it was still having an impact on all kinds of folks. I was in the zone.

Bertice in Prison

But I digress. I was telling you about the comedy circuit. I finally escaped Canada, and through Mark and Robin Hellman, whose agency I signed with, I was booked on another college tour. But whereas Zoe had cast her net across all of Canada, the Hellmans worked one section of the United States at a time, which resulted in a pace I could sustain. The Hellmans saw the purpose behind my humor and were helping me spread the word.

My new agents even got me bookings at prisons. Talk about a captive audience (come on, you knew that was coming). I'd had guts aplenty before, but being inside prisons made me tougher and gave me a new appreciation of my freedom.

I created new routines for the prisons and impressed the inmates with my ability to pick up their lingo. One suggested it came easily because I had a lot of relatives on the inside. "No," I told him, "but they should be."

I joked with the transvestites and told them I was pissed that they looked better than I did. I made fun of the guards and said they resembled a picture I'd seen at the post office. They all loved it.

I loved it that I was seen as a positive role model. I encouraged the inmates to read and then get their asses out of there. I told them that *we* needed them to change, and to grow.

Soon I began to get even more bookings. I'd do stand-up and then be booked for a lecture afterward. And then for four years running I received the National Association of Campus Activities Comedian of the Year award, Lecturer of the Year award, and/or Entertainer of the Year award. The colleges are a wonderful place to perform. The audiences were bright, and on the fringe of everything real. Afterward we'd chat for hours. Students enabled me to realize a trend before it happened. I was also able to have an impact on the lives of young people who had the potential to change their world.

I loved what I was doing, but I grew frustrated that though

I was getting my message across, I was still doing it only one person at a time. My divorce was about to be final and I knew that it was time for some other changes in my life. I had begun to understand the power of the media and decided it was time to tap it.

What's a Nice Girl Like You Doing in a Business Like This?

Star public relations agent David Brokaw was doing work for Bill Cosby and other big-name clients. The Hellmans had heard about his work and contacted him about me. This was during a time when *The Cosby Show* was the number-one show on television. Even though David was extremely busy, he said that he'd be honored to represent me.

I started investing in my career—the old Protestant Ethic in the Spirit of Capitalism. I got new pictures and a classier wardrobe, and had a new tape of my performances made. With my new power publicist, I was on the way. I figured that I would devote another year to comedy before I made a decision about what to do next.

Within two months I was flooded with offers. In addition to talk about a sitcom, a late-nighter, and a variety show, I was offered a deal hosting my own talk show. Then another offer came in. And then another. I was being blessed with the opportunity to choose.

I selected Twentieth Television, a division of 20th Century–Fox, over several other competing syndicators. When I met with the folks at Twentieth, I immediately liked them for several reasons. First of all, they were about to make Lucy Salhany the first woman president of a network. She was tough and struck fear in the hearts of the men who worked for her. She had worked her way up in a business that has a limited view of women, and she was good.

I was also impressed that the executives directly in charge of my show seemed to share my vision for a positive, clean program. Like me, they believed that real folks could be sensational. At least that's what they told me at the time. While my career as a television personality seemed inevitable, I never stopped doing lectures or stand-up. I realized that being directly in touch with my audiences, particularly college audiences, had helped to get me to television and that staying in touch would keep me there.

Other syndicators bid for my show along with Twentieth, though later they publicly said they'd turned it down. In Hollywood no one wants to admit that they lose anything, so they lie about it. Many of them had even offered me more money than Twentieth, but they weren't willing to give me any creative control, nor did I feel they wanted a clean show. But at least they were up front.

A syndicator sells rights to a show to the highest bidder in each market, which means that a syndicated program can appear on a CBS affiliate in Boston, an NBC station in Tallahassee, and an independent station in Seattle. But thanks to a hardworking sales team and promotional spots put together by Kevin Burns, the show became the fastest-selling talk show in the history of syndication.

Steve Clemmens and Ramey Warren, my then enthusiastic coexecutive producers for our pilot programs, were replaced by Bonnie Kaplan, whose experience in daytime television was vast: If there was a talk show she hadn't worked on, that show would never admit it. She brought in Sol Feldman as senior producer.

The talk-show format is grueling and unlike any other. We'd tape two shows a day, three or four times a week, sometimes more. On the days when we weren't taping, we were preparing for future shows, booking and interviewing guests, planning the order of the shows, arranging for audiences who had an interest in the topic of the day. There was one woman who came to practically every show. We started calling her our own Mrs. Miller (as in Merv Griffin, you young things).

Because we'd only done six pilot shows to pitch with—most other new programs generated around twenty to forty—we were behind from the beginning. On top of that pressure, I suddenly found myself with three children.

I also had to deal with a few other distractions, the kind that wear Gucci loafers and fly in first-class from the coast to check on their investment. People assume that the goal of mass media is to inform and entertain. Naively, I did, too. But what I discovered was that the goal of television and all mass media is first and foremost to make money. That's probably why there are so many talk shows on the air: They are inexpensive to produce, and successful ones make millions of dollars. When my show first aired, it's true we weren't the instant breakout hit that some people had predicted. But it's also true that we entered the market with better ratings than many shows that had been on for years.

Unfortunately, to many of our executive "buddies," this meant we were a failure, and they never let us forget it. They criticized everything we did and never acknowledged that we'd done a good job given the time and resources we had at our disposal. My would-be hairdresser/executive—you remember the one I mean—was in this crowd.

To be fair, some executives didn't feel this way, and they were instrumental in helping us get better and in keeping us up. If it hadn't been for them, I might have quit and moved to my sister/friend Bernita's family farm in Georgia to help slop the hogs.

What I did instead was to ask Bernita to move to Chicago and join the show as our coordinating producer. Soon, Bonnie, who had just had a baby, left to be a full-time mother; Sol took over as executive producer, with Karen Molamed becoming senior producer.

We worked literally around the clock. I had to summon the joy of Sister Evangelist Lucille Treadway, the pride of Mrs. Dorsey, and the determination of Lucy Salhany to keep going. Most days, Karen, Bernita, and I didn't leave the office until after midnight; Sol usually slept there, showering in my dressing room and keeping spare clothes in a desk drawer.

I've never met a more dedicated, creative individual than Sol. I don't believe I ever will. Sol is Jewish (like the name Sol Feldman could be anything but), and he's also a comedy writer and one of the funniest people on the planet. He would crack us up with stories about his French mother, who could somehow connect simple events like her daughter's forbidden use of perfume to the invasion of the Nazis and the horrors of fascism.

Karen's nutty family stories, Bernita's tales of life in Ludowici, and Bonnie's ability to relate anything to a shopping experience became the necessary distractions that kept us sane.

During that year of taping the show, I don't really know how we kept it together. In addition to the shows we taped, we also had to handle the thousands of letters and calls from people who wanted my help. They all said that they could tell I cared and just knew that I'd help them. We wept for all that we knew we couldn't do, but we were determined to always do our best.

204

If You Can't Cry, Laugh

The executives kept turning up the pressure on us to produce sleazy and malicious shows. Under the circumstances, I wasn't surprised when one guest on another show murdered a second guest; I was only surprised it took so long.

I didn't give in to that pressure, but I did work hard to cooperate with the network honchos. When they told us to do a remote from a strip joint, Bonnie came up with the idea to make it a contest between pros and amateurs. The staff found homemakers, mechanics, and teachers to play the parts, and we booked a panel of celebrity judges that included Mother Love, Morton Downey Jr., and Charo.

We had a ball. I did my own dance, but because of a music mix-up, instead of "Big Spender" I was dancing to some slow ballad. It was even more hilarious. We learned to approach more shows in the same manner, turning instructions we didn't like to the show's advantage. Instead of either getting into huge fights with Hollywood or coming up with on-air sleaze spectaculars, we had fun, and so did the audiences.

As a talk-show host you get to hear all kinds of terrible stories. This could have ended up making us feel totally exhausted, but we chose to channel our frustration positively. Frequently, staff members even took up collections for certain guests, and we made it a practice to do follow-ups, calling past guests to see how they were doing. We hired baby-sitters for couples who were having problems and could have used time alone together more than time in therapy. We found a new home for a woman and her children and even provided the first two months' rent.

You See Bad, I See Good

In the end, we had to be content with that kind of personal gratification, because Twentieth Television decided to cancel us and contacted the press before they even told us. Naturally, we were upset, but at the same time we were relieved. We'd been working for months without any word of renewal, and at least now we knew.

Ultimately, Twentieth Television's president, Greg Meidel, flew to Chicago to tell us that he was sorry, but the decision was final. We were grateful that he came in person, and some of us actually believed that he took it harder than we did. There are few class people working in television, but Greg is definitely one of them.

Ask me why we were canceled. Just go ahead, ask.

I don't know.

Sure, we had been shifted to lesser time slots in some markets, but even then, our ratings went up. The show that replaced us still has not come up to our numbers.

All of this is still a mystery to me, and if I didn't have anything else to do, I'd solve it.

I do know that I had the satisfaction of meeting the challenge I'd set for myself and my show: having a positive impact on the lives of viewers by being entertaining and informative without compromising my integrity. We'd done that.

I've always enjoyed working and always will, but I'm still learning to be picky and to only accept work that is good for me. I am also learning to work with those who respect my calling, who want to grow as I do, and who will lead me in the right direction.

God doesn't want any less for me, so who am I to argue?

I can't say that I would have wished for everything that happened to me on *The Bertice Berry Show*, but then again I wouldn't have wished for everything that happened in my childhood either. But it's all made me who I am, and that's something I'm happy about.

Sometimes what's supposed to be bad can turn out to be good.

CHAPTER EIGHT

Beauty's Only Soul Deep

I'll never look like Barbie.

Besides, she's plastic. Her chest is too big and her waist is too small. If a real person were built like that, she'd fall right over.

We live in a society that spends more on cosmetics than education. This is devastating. Instead of spending millions of dollars to look like someone else, I've decided to work on changing people's attitudes so they can think like me for free.

*I*t's always been hard for me to feel beautiful, but it's something I had to do. As a feminist, I want to believe that a woman's looks are secondary to her abilities. But I also want a million dollars a day, a gorgeous man to massage my feet, and, oh, yeah, world peace. I've had to struggle to like and accept myself because I still live in the real world, a world that gives little girls Barbie dolls to play with.

Everyone has a natural inner beauty, but this beauty can't be projected until we accept who we are.

While other girls were spending hours in front of a mirror, I was running past them, afraid to see the reflection of the ugly little Black girl. I never looked at *Young Miss* or other teen glamour magazines. The image of the beautiful girls in those magazines was as cruel a sight to me as seeing myself in the mirror.

Since I knew I would never be the pretty one, I got to be the smart and funny one. Then it became okay for me to look in the mirror. In fact, I started to use it as a tool to practice my funny faces, and I had some great ones.

Now ugliness was no longer a curse—it was a talent.

I remember being told by an aunt that I should study hard and learn a lot, because boys who were going to be somebody wouldn't want me. Therefore, she said, I should try to be somebody for myself.

At the time, I focused on the part about not being attractive, and I desperately wanted to be attractive. I didn't really hear the part about being somebody for myself. Only later did I realize how much I had taken these words to heart.

A Girl Called Gip

People were always telling me that I should lose weight. They never said how much, just that I should do it. They said it as if they were the first to think of it. As if it were easy, like changing my shoes. They might as well have said, "Be White." They have pills for that, too, don't they?

When I was fourteen, I had a checkup with the school doctor. He told me I was obese. *Obese.* I wasn't quite sure what the word meant. So I looked it up in the dictionary.

Obese . . . Bertice . . . grossly overweight. I hadn't felt *grossly* overweight. As a matter of fact, people had often told me I was light on my feet. But then, when you think about it, that's not a compliment often paid to skinny people. It's like being called articulate. No one ever says that about White folks. Whenever I open my mouth, people proclaim, "Oh, my, she's so articulate."

Since most of the women in my family and in my church are large, my weight was as normal to me as my skin color, but other people didn't seem to be as accepting. In addition, the doctor informed me that I had high blood pressure, and unless I did something about it, I was at risk for a stroke or heart attack. Since my mother had had two heart attacks before she was age sixty, and my grandmother Caroline had died from a stroke, his warning did not fall on deaf ears.

But I still didn't take this health risk all that seriously. Among other things, I didn't want my brothers to be right. They had diagnosed my condition long before any visit to the doctor. They'd said I was fat.

My brothers had nicknamed me Pig, a name they called me at the most inopportune times, like in front of my friends at school, or during those rare times when our telephone was connected and people would call me at home. I came running when they shouted, *"Pig! Telephone!"*

When my mother finally made them stop, they got creative and started calling me Gip. If you're dyslexic, you know what that's a nickname for.

I could count on my brothers to make grunting noises whenever I walked across the room, and to say all of the mean things that brothers like to say to sisters no matter what they look like. They would make sniffing noises and ask one another, "Do you smell bacon? I smell bacon . . . or is it ham hocks?" Believe it or not, I learned to accept this. It hurt a great deal, but I wasn't going to let them know. It's amazing to me now to think of how much time I spent putting up with their insults when I could've been working on how to accept myself just the way I was.

I'm a Vegetarian; I Don't Eat Anything That Has a Mother

Sometimes what's intended to be bad can turn out to be good.

Whenever I ate pork, my brothers would call me a cannibal. Choked with laughter, they'd entertain each other with jokes at my expense: "Look, it's a pig eating a pig." This insult would be repeated as if for the first time every time we had pork.

Without really thinking about it, eventually I stopped eating pork. By that time my brothers had moved on to another animal. The insults now centered on beef. "Look, it's a cow eating a cow," they'd merrily observe. I stopped eating beef. Now I had only chicken and vegetables left.

One Thanksgiving, my brother Kevin made a feeble attempt at a stuffing joke, but the thrill was gone. Inadvertently I had found a way to stop the jokes and become healthier, too. All the animal jokes had driven me to become a vegetarian.

I was one of those people who ate less than everyone else, but still couldn't lose any weight. From the time I was in high school until I finished college, I was always on some kind of diet. First I'd eat nothing but grapefruit, then nothing but lettuce. I did more damage to my body than good. First I'd lose weight, lots of it. Then I'd gain twice the amount that I had lost.

I have always been heavier than I look, but that's not a compliment. I'm only five feet two inches, but at my heaviest I got up to 250 pounds. When I realized how much I weighed, I was in shock. Really. I couldn't move. All of a sudden, I felt the weight of those 200-plus pounds.

When I was growing up, I didn't have boyfriends. I told myself that I didn't want them. I told myself I was serving God. I may have been serving God, but you know that sign at McDonald's that says "Over three billion served"? I was two of them. And then when they added chicken to their menu, I was born again.

It wasn't how much I ate, it was what I was eating and when I was eating it. We church folks had services that went late into the night. Afterward we'd cram ourselves into someone's car and go to Denny's. I know what you're thinking. Denny's doesn't serve Black people. But think about it. It's midnight. You're the manager. And six fat people come in. What are you going to do?

I'd eat a meal of chicken and french fries, coleslaw and corn, buttered rolls and a half gallon of ice tea—sweetened with Sweet'n Low, of course.

I envied the looks that other young women got from men when they walked down the street, even though I told myself that I was glad not to be degraded that way. Instead, I got a different kind of attention. People made fun of my large hips and behind and would say cruel things like, "You could carry a tray on that thing."

To escape the taunts, I turned inward. I forgot about what I looked like and started to focus on my mental and spiritual development. I discovered that women who see themselves as physically unappealing can be powerful in other ways. The invisibility of being ignored and treated like a nonperson enabled me to observe men without being observed, like the spook who sat by the door. I collected a lot of wisdom that way.

In college, men always came to me with their "woman problems," as if I weren't a woman myself. They'd say things like, "Okay, say you're a girl and I'm attracted to you, but you don't notice me. What should I do?" They'd talk to me as if I'd been spayed, but I never protested. I'd help them find solutions and promptly return to my own loneliness.

My male friends told me all the things they liked in a woman. She should be funny and smart, sensitive, and able to listen to them as a friend. She should also understand basketball, but still hold them as a lover. Even though I had all the qualities they described, I knew I'd never be on their list.

Men and women say that they want one thing, but then often go looking for another. "My man should be smart, sensitive, and caring and have a desire to change the world." "My woman should have a sense of humor, an easy disposition, and like to take long walks in the park."

But nobody means it.

I wish people would just loudly admit, "First and foremost, I want someone who looks *good*. Someone everyone else in the world is lusting after but can't have, because she's mine. Ha! Ha! Ha! She's mine!" People should be honest about their urges and their desire to possess.

As difficult as those fat-girl years were, I learned to love myself. I decided one day that I was fat and so what. I told myself that if the average American was overweight, then I wasn't overweight—I was average. I recognized that designers were not making clothes with me in mind. I wouldn't alter my body for a piece of clothing; instead, I'd buy clothing that fit.

This attitude developed in two stages. First, I decided that there was someone for everyone. I figured out that some people actually liked my size. Whenever I walked by older men, I'd hear them say things like, "Aw, sukay sukay now." When I visited the Virgin Islands or Greece or practically anyplace where they don't speak English, I discovered that women my size were considered beautiful.

In museums I looked at the works of Titian, Rubens, Rodin, and other artists and saw that the women who captivated them were not the women who made the *Sports Illustrated* swimsuit issue. You tell me whose art will endure longer.

I began to see that it was White male standards of beauty that said I was unattractive. Well, who died and made them beauty consultants?

I started to leaf through my stack of glamour magazines with a different perspective. The tables were turned when I became the standard of measurement: The models now seemed way too pale and way too thin, their features identical to one another's. In comparison, I was magnificent.

What I had once thought of as flaws, I now saw as the things that made me beautiful, that set me apart from the crowd. I knew then that I didn't want hair that blew in the wind. I wanted hair that greeted the sun. I wanted a behind that allowed my clothes to follow me and not the other way around. I decided my skin testified to the brilliance of my people, and my lips made my love want more.

My pastor used to tell the parable of the ugly duck:

> *There was once a duck who looked like a duck. But one day she saw a swan and thought that the swan was the most beautiful thing she had ever seen.*
>
> *The duck decided that she wanted to look like the swan, so she set out to do this. She did swan aerobics and went to swan finishing school. She even underwent swan plastic surgery.*
>
> *And she did it. She became a beautiful swan.*
>
> *And then, one day, as if by magic, she met the man of her dreams, but he only liked ducks.*

When I first heard this story, it was like a gift. I could be myself because out there was someone who would want the fat, smart, funny Bertice. I'd save this fat for him.

The initial impact of the parable began to wear off as I realized that the moral of the story was not about what I wanted. It was about what some unknown fairy-tale man wanted. I needed to find and express my own standards, to like myself independent of whether the men in my life liked ducks.

I'm somewhat ashamed to admit it, but for a while I was the only beautiful person on the planet. I'd look at a couple that I'd previously thought of as attractive and tell myself, they're so ugly, they deserve each other.

Looking back, this perspective seems as ill-informed as the way I'd been treated. But it was also self-preservation. I had to do it. I needed to erase what was really someone else's definition of beauty and replace it with my own before I could truly accept myself.

I began to marvel at the curves of my large hips, to enjoy the fact that I had a place to rest my hand when I wanted to give attitude. I thought of my behind as a large, wonderful pillow, a place where my future love could rest.

I started standing taller, which made me feel taller. I ignored the trends and the clothes that models wore and looked for things that flattered me, clothes that flowed where my body did and cinched my small waist. Suddenly men were asking me why I was covering up my "asset." I'd cleverly reply that loose clothing and a man's imagination were always sexier than a tight pair of jeans.

Once I started to feel beautiful, I began to crave more physical activity. I wanted to be out where people could see me, instead of staying hidden behind a book or a church pew, so I went for a lot of walks. Soon I began to speed-walk every morning and to play racquetball.

I attacked racquetball with the same hunger I had attacked books and midnight meals at Denny's, and I quickly became good at it. I even began to run, something I had never done before unless a dog was chasing me.

The more I exercised, the more my body rebelled against the junk and pollutants that I'd been feeding it. Over a seven-year period, I gradually eliminated them all. I became more selective than ever about what I ate. I wouldn't eat anything with ingredients I couldn't pronounce. I got so conscientious that the only thing I could buy from the grocery store was water in glass bottles. I bought only organic fruits and vegetables.

This wasn't as easy as it sounds. I was living in Kent, Ohio, where organic produce was about as hard to find as a Black man.

By the time I consciously realized what I was doing, I had already lost about sixty pounds. My friends didn't recognize me, nor did they remember me as being as large as I had been. They looked at old pictures of me in amazement and said, "That's not you. You were never *that* big."

After I lost weight, things changed. The guys who'd been my buddies and had come to me for advice were coming to me for dates. My female friends, who had never been bothered by the time I spent with their boyfriends ("It's just Bert," they'd say), were now jealous of the time we'd spend together. They'd say, "Oh, she think she's cute now," or, "Who does she think she is? She was nicer when she was fat."

One woman on campus actually passed around an old picture of me fat. On the back of the picture she wrote, "The Real Bertice."

The problems that people had with me after I lost weight were theirs, not mine. I knew that if I regained the weight, things would go back to "normal." But I knew I would never be fat again. Pleasingly plump, maybe, but never fat.

After the first sixty pounds came off, I lost a little more each year. Not only was this measured approach less of a shock to my body, it was less of a shock to my spirit and the spirits of those around me. Today I weigh less than the lie on my driver's license.

I've learned a great deal more about my body and have discovered I have an unusually slow metabolism. To compensate, I exercise a lot. In the early 1980s, before gyms were the pickup joints that they are today, there were only a few women in the gym who were serious weight lifters or bodybuilders, and I became one of them. Most of the other women at the gym were just trying to lose a few pounds before bikini season. They wore color-coordinated outfits and lots of makeup.

I started helping other women—the ones who were there to exercise—train for bodybuilding competitions. I got up early in the morning to run with them, and then I trained with them in the afternoon. We'd work chests and backs one day, legs and arms the next. I helped them by choreographing their posing routines, and soon the men wanted my help, too.

I never really considered competing myself, but I secretly fantasized about being in a string bikini, all oiled up, muscles bulging. The announcer would say, "Can you believe that just a few short months ago, this lean, mean fighting machine was obese? Ladies and gentlemen, that means grossly overweight."

My body will never look like Twiggy's or Halle Berry's. Thank God! (*Did you see Halle Berry in* The Flintstones? *Was she miscast or what? Where's Jackee when you need her?*) I've grown to love my body. I no longer need to feel superior. But I know I am.

Black Is Truly Beautiful

Today I walked past a mirror and saw this gorgeous woman. "Wow," she looks good, I thought to myself. Then I realized that the woman was me.

—*Journal entry, December 11, 1991*

My black features were like a puzzle, and the pieces didn't fit. Not in a White world. My nose was too large, my eyes were too big, and my skin was too dark.

When I was in grade school, an artist visited our class and showed us a painting of a little Black boy. I thought the boy was ugly, but the artist didn't. He asked me what I thought of the little boy, and I told him I thought the child was ugly.

"That's funny," he said, "because of all the children here, I think he looks most like you."

The other kids laughed but I was crushed. Even though these were the Black Is Beautiful days, I hadn't gotten the message.

I prayed to be light-skinned. I was quick to join in when my siblings teased my brother Brent about his dark skin. I didn't like being called Burnt-ice and Butt-ice. I wanted to be one of the pretty girls. But I could only be the funny girl, the church girl, the girl who read books. Those books saved my sanity and made me beautiful in spite of what the world said. In them, I found characters who looked like me and felt like I did. I wasn't alone.

When I took my mother to see the movie *The Color Purple,* she said that when I was young I looked like the little girl who played Nettie. "That's funny," I told her. "I remember feeling like and looking like Celie."

People also said that my teeth were yellow, so I hardly ever smiled. Before I got my permanent teeth, I had a tremendous overbite. One day while we were playing, someone pushed me from behind and rammed my face into a metal fire escape. My front teeth were knocked out and my nose was broken.

When I came home bloody and screaming, my mother washed me up, gave me two aspirins, and put me to bed. My mother had no medical insurance. I'm sure she prayed, because she always did, and that was it.

When my teeth grew back in, they were much straighter. People assume that I've had braces or that my teeth are capped. I tell them that I had poor people's surgery: We just left them alone and trusted God.

How Can Hair Be Bad?

I've worn my hair natural for as long as I can remember. People often told me that I needed to get it "fixed," as if it had been broken or something. I hated my sandy red bush that was always unruly.

My sister Chris recently told me how she used to love to wash my hair. She said that when she'd lean me over the sink and grab my hair by the handfuls, she felt as if she held the sun in her hands. I wish she'd told me then.

Anyway, as I got older, my hair got darker, and it also got shorter. Like most Black girls, I was constantly combing it. I combed it so much that at one point it began to break off in handfuls.

A girl named Tracey Morgan had the best hairstyle of all the girls in my school, mostly because her mother owned Wilmington's most popular Black hair salon. Tracey and her mother felt my hair needed work, and Mrs. Morgan offered to give me a free relaxer.

I was so excited. I was seventeen and most girls I knew were already making regular visits to the beauty parlor, but my family hadn't been able to afford such luxuries. I couldn't wait to take Mrs. Morgan up on her offer and quickly booked a Saturday appointment.

I had never been to a salon before and was impressed by the sink with the dip in it. You could just sit back and have someone wash your hair for you. This was a far cry from pressing up against the kitchen sink with Chris's weight on my back.

When the relaxer was applied to my nappy hair, it burned, which surprised me. I also wondered why Tracey's mom had to wear gloves to apply something that was sitting that close to my brain. When I asked, Mrs. Morgan told me that the relaxer had lye in it.

In science class we'd conducted an experiment with lye. "Be extra careful," the teacher had explained. "Lye can burn you. Don't get any on your hands, and don't let it spill on you, or it could burn right through your jeans." I reflected on this as I sat in the chair at the salon, wondering what I had subjected myself to and hoping it was worth it.

When I saw the results, I decided that the burning, the fear, and the long wait were definitely worth it. I was beautiful! I looked like the other newly permed church girls, who'd shake their heads a little harder than usual and yell, "Hal-le-lu-jah!" tossing their hair with each syllable. Hal-le-lu-jah. My hair could move and blow in the wind like a White person's.

I skipped all the way home and couldn't wait until Saturday morning service. As soon as they saw me, I noticed people were treating me special. After church, practically everyone had some backhanded compliment to offer me.

"It's about time you did something with your head."

"Girl, you look almost human."

"Now, if you could only do something about that butt."

I took it all in stride and said, "Yeah, and Jesus loves you, too."

Nothing could get me down. I had been to a salon and now I had "good" hair.

That week in school I was a pest. I went around saying things like, "My beautician says I have a good grade of hair," and "My beautician says I have to come back in two weeks." I had only been to the place once, and I hadn't even been a paying customer. But I was walking and acting like a regular.

I figured those who didn't say anything about my hair were

just jealous. For some reason, this made me feel better. Why is it that folks feel good when we think others feel bad?

Eventually, my virgin naps started to grow in, and much faster than I had anticipated. My permed hair was even more fragile than my hair had been before and broke off with alarming frequency. I knew then how victims of RioHair Products feel now.

Without the funds to fix my hair or get a touch-up, I was forced to return to the pulled-back pigtail I had worn preperm. My loving family and Christian friends made the negative comments that I had come to expect.

"Uh-huh, we knew it wasn't going to last for long."

"You should get it done again. You were beautiful before."

It's amazing how people can give you a compliment after it no longer applies.

It was a few years before I could afford to return to the salon chair. When I did, I had to listen to jokes about the differences between a White woman's flowing hair and a Black woman's short naps. "When a White woman brushes her hair," the most popular one went, "she brushes long strokes and the brush sings 'Nearer my God to Thee, nearer to Thee.' But when a Black woman does it, it just says, 'Near, near.'" Everyone would laugh, as if the joke wasn't about them.

I had to do something with my hair, so I learned to braid it in cornrows. When cornrows became popular, I already had them. Still, when I had enough money, I went right back to the salon and permed my hair a few more times. But I soon grew tired of combing my hair every day, so I went back to braiding.

I couldn't believe all the time women in college spent on the outside of their heads, as if to say, "I gotta look good, y'all. I gota test to fail."

At one point, I spent a few months teaching in the U.S. Virgin Islands, and there I discovered dreadlocks. My friend and colleague Cassandra Dunn wore them and asked me when I planned to *lock up*. I loved her thick, nappy locks and knew that it would only be a matter of time before I had my own. By now I didn't even want to take the time to unbraid and rebraid my hair every five weeks. I don't know how women do otherwise every day, and I sure don't know why.

Dreadlocks were even less acceptable to the usual naysayers than my braids had been. Even today people assume that everyone who wears them is a part of the Rastafarian movement and/or doesn't bathe.

On the day that I returned to Ohio, I took out my cornrows and plaited my hair in lots of tiny braids. I know the number, but you're really not supposed to count them—some old superstition. I allowed those braids to grow into locks, then I cut the ends off.

I knew that folks would find my new hair hard to accept, but I wasn't prepared for the full force of the negative reactions. People called me Buckwheat and even laughed right in my face. Strangers came up to me and asked, with real concern, "Why did you do that to yourself?"

Some people tried to impress me with their firsthand knowledge of my hair. They advised me on how to care for and style it, even though my hair was as close as they'd ever gotten to dreadlocks.

When I started my locks, Whoopi Goldberg wasn't yet a household name. Dreadlock wearers had no role models. We weren't in Nike ads or on cereal boxes. We certainly weren't in the White House. The most I could hope for was the occasional visiting reggae band.

My mother acted as if I had deliberately tried to hurt her. She wondered aloud why her child was so strange. People would ask, "How are you ever going to get a job with that hair?" "I guess on my abilities," I'd reply.

Eventually, I learned to tune out the criticism and accept my natural hair. Once I accepted my hair, my nose and lips were not far behind. I started to smile more, and when I danced, I threw my head like the wild woman everyone thought I was.

I surrounded myself with images of people who looked like me. Even my picture of Jesus is of a Black man with dreadlocks. It makes sense. It validates my existence in the same way that the White Christ with blue eyes and blond hair is validating for some White folks. Besides, mine's got to be closer to the truth: How could anyone believe that it was some milky-white Christ who walked through the desert with a comb.

I noticed that the more I embraced my looks, the more others embraced them, too. A self previously hidden by my lack of self-esteem began to burst forth. And I loved her fiercely.

Amazingly, others started to copy my look. My friends seemed to recognize how liberating locks are, and today at least thirty of my friends and family members wear them. In fact, when the TV executive tried to get me to get rid of my dreadlocks, my family members rallied in support of my hair, which they themselves had once disliked. They showed their solidarity by locking their own.

"We don't die, we multiply," Chris said.

You See Chopped Liver, I See Pâté

I have a friend named Gail. Gail is a White woman who's slightly heavy. At one time she felt unattractive because of it.

She'd complain and make faces about the lack of available men. When I told her to forget about them and be happy with my company, she immediately knew what I meant.

Many times we'd go out dancing, and guys would ask, "Did you come alone?" I'd tell them that I'd come with my friend and point to Gail. They'd look at me as if I were some alien and ask again, this time a little louder, "So you came alone?"

Gail and I often laughed about this and would call one another chopped liver. Gradually, Gail began to accept herself as she was, and she experienced a real sense of liberation. Meantime, back on the dance floor, we stopped waiting for a man to ask us to dance and would instead rush to the floor together, dancing wildly.

Once a guy came up and sort of pushed me. "Are you some kind of lesbian?" he asked. I remembered a joke I'd heard a woman comic tell and answered, "No, but if you're the alternative, I'll try it."

When my cousin Robin moved to Chicago, she and my friend Dorann and I would all go out. We're all larger than a model type, and we all wear it well. Robin exudes sensuality, and even though she is "queen-sized," she leaves men breathless. I liked to watch men watch her, knowing they couldn't understand their sudden attraction to a larger woman.

Dorann is equally beautiful, with very dark skin and deep-set eyes. She has the same effect on men, especially when she laughs. I realized a long time ago that when I enter a room with beautiful people like Robin and Dorann, I always feel more beautiful myself.

I have a friend who felt uncomfortable with her looks. Ironically, she is light-skinned, had permed hair, and was very thin. She was the spitting image of the self I had wished for so long ago.

Mary Louise always held her head down and kept her arms at her sides. When she sat, she'd clasp her hands between her knees and barely look up.

All of Mary Louise's sisters wore their hair in short Afros, and I asked her why she didn't. She said that she had wanted to but had been afraid. "Of what?" I asked. She didn't know.

I took her to a salon and dared her to cut her hair. She did, and was absolutely stunning. It was ironic to me that I had been wanting to look like her, while she was trying to find her natural looks—looks that were closer to mine. Mary Louise also said that she was uncomfortable with her name. She said she never felt like a Mary Louise. I started to call her Nia, which is Swahili for "purpose." She eventually took it as her name. Nia now enters a room with her head thrown back and a huge smile on her face.

She learned the same thing I did—a woman's purpose is not hidden in her beauty.

Her beauty is hidden in her purpose.

Once I had accepted my calling in life and learned to enjoy it, my natural beauty emerged. I was still uncomfortable when people flattered me; I couldn't get used to it, and I thought they must want something from me. Once I became comfortable with myself and their compliments, I started to enjoy being pretty.

A Feminist Wears Makeup

Up until my early thirties I'd never worn makeup. I felt that makeup was somehow antifeminist—that it was another trap, another male conspiracy designed to keep me busy so I wouldn't have time for more important concerns.

But at some point I realized that being a feminist didn't mean that I had to reject things that were feminine.

No one helped me with this conclusion more than my friend and makeup artist Earl Nicholson. Earl is a beautiful and quiet Black man whose spirit and laughter could lift me from any state of sadness.

I met Earl in the department store where he worked. I was buying a present in another department, but Earl offered his help anyway. Afterward, we shook hands, and he held mine for a while and in a sincere voice told me that if he could ever do anything for me, he'd be glad to do it. When I left the store, I thought, What a wonderful soul.

Earl and I didn't know anything about each other except for our names. The following week, my friend Bonnie Kaplan, a talk-show producer, gave me a list of recommendations for makeup artists. Earl's name was at the top.

I immediately remembered him and hired him on the spot.

I was afraid to sit in makeup chairs. Whenever I'd had makeup "professionally" applied for television appearances, I felt like a French prostitute—or maybe it was Russian. Whatever the case, it wasn't me afterward.

Artists would use dark liner on the inside of my lips to make them look smaller, apply foundation that was too light for my skin, and contour my nose in an attempt to make it appear thinner. In other words, they tried to make me look White. I had finally accepted my looks, and now they were being altered for mass consumption.

But when Earl did my makeup, he was gentle and worked me into it gradually. Instead of covering or modifying my looks, he created a style that complemented and enhanced them. He showed me that makeup didn't have to be a conspiracy!

Earl's work made me think of the makeup artistry of the ancient Egyptians and the spiritual ceremonies that I thought were in some ways similar to what was being done to me. Those long-ago people were being prepared for celebrational dances, sacred missions, sometimes for battle. I, too, was being prepared to fight my own battles, and I felt I was already an experienced warrior.

I no longer fight with my looks or the curves of my body. I try to eat foods that are good for me. I don't drink alcohol or take any drugs—well, with the exception of medicine for cramps.

Occasionally I'll eat macaroni and cheese, and once a year I'll eat a piece of Miss Nellie Boykin's fried chicken. I may even skip a day of exercise here and there. But I've come to realize that the paths to beauty and well-being are interrelated and continuous. There are no quick-fix perms and no miracle cures. Cinderella exists only in fairy tales, and for this I am grateful.

Loving and embracing myself is as necessary to me as breathing, and as I've discovered, beauty and freedom go hand in hand.

CHAPTER NINE

Spiritual Warrior

God is neither male nor female. She is a spirit and we must worship Her in spirit and in truth.

But when I pray to God, She answers because She's Black.

*U*ntil very recently in our history, most people have been denied access to formal education. People of color, women, and poor people are, in many ways, still being denied this access. I think this is why they tend to be more spiritual people. The mind always yearns for a way to make sense of things. When you are denied access to answers that make sense, your soul will take over, seeking out explanations wherever possible.

It's been the burden or the blessing of the underprivileged to be the spiritual warriors of this society. It's usually the women of the family who make sure that everyone goes to church, and that the children get to Sunday school. Blacks have always had to march and ask God for equality. *Poor people have always had to pray for everything.* Toni Morrison once said that it was the task of the oppressed to teach the oppressor. This is true, but I wonder, At what point do the oppressors start to educate themselves?

Those who have had access to formal education have often been denied access to that which is spiritual. They've been taught to reject that which they cannot see or explain. For many, God does not exist in any form. The world is explained in scientific terms; there is no time or need for soul searching.

Self-evaluation exists only to increase one's scientific knowledge or monetary worth.

Is there room for both? Can an informal education coexist with a formal one? Can a person who relies on science for understanding trust God for wisdom? Absolutely! I have spent twenty-two years of my life in school. But my education did not start or end there. My educational process is both formal and informal. It is spiritual and scientific.

Okay. I've been hitting you over the head with the determination business and the hard-work stuff. You're probably wondering if I'm made of steel.

I am woman. Hear me snore!

I try to keep going, but sometimes I get tired, I get weary. It's always something. If it's not a business complication or something horrible I read in the newspapers, it's a friend who's in trouble again or one of my kids just being too eager to do something before his or her time.

Sometimes I'm able to turn on that extra little bit of drive and say, "Keep on, Bertice." I've been fortunate to have had many good friends who've held my hand or kicked my butt, depending on what was needed.

But the real comfort, the real resilience, comes from my faith in God and Her love for me.

So pay attention, because I've saved the stuff I really want you to remember for last.

Give Me Shelter

My mother had been forced to attend church as a child; it was a chore for her. If she didn't go, just as if she didn't scrub the floors, she got punished. She took us kids to church off and on before she began what church folks called her backsliding. Once she saw a few suspicious looks, she said that church folks didn't know what they were missing and gave up.

But church became a refuge for me. The Mother Church of Christ in Wilmington was home to me when I was afraid of my own home. Family friend Barbara Dorsey had invited me to attend, and because I could fondly recall the peaceful services we had attended before my mother started drinking, I accepted.

What the people at the Mother Church of Christ had was something very different from what they had at the prim church I had known in my early childhood. This was an active church whose members worshiped an active God, whom they believed had healed them or moved them from the path of an oncoming truck. Their Jesus was a friend, a brother.

They also believed strongly in the Holy Ghost. The spirit would fall on them and they'd run around the church dancing and crying. They also spoke with other tongues, one of the many gifts of the spirit that was first experienced by early Christians on the Day of Pentecost.

Some people don't believe in tongues, but I've actually witnessed some incredible things. I've seen people get "a word" from God in some unknown language, and others become suddenly able to interpret that foreign-sounding "word."

One night when we were in prayer service, a man came into our church from off the street. He was a little shabby-looking, but then so were a lot of our members. Someone stood up and started speaking in tongues, and then someone else interpreted. The message being delivered was that this stranger was there to steal.

The visitor stood up and began to cry. He said it was true that he intended to steal—he said he and his family were very hungry. So we church folks prayed for him and then sent for his family so that they could eat with us. (No, we didn't just give him money; we were spiritual, but we weren't dumb.)

This kind of thing might send some people running right out the door, but it drew me in. I felt right at home.

Talkin' to Yourself Is Fine

It's still somewhat hard for me to tell people about this, but it's something my family has always known about me. I used to talk to myself. At least that's what they thought. But I wasn't really talking to myself. I have always, with the exception of a few short periods in my life, been able to see things and hear voices. Sometimes I see people or animals; sometimes I just see shadows or silhouettes.

I didn't realize until later that Black folks and many other people have long traditions in which "unseen" presences are as real as the ones everybody sees. These images and "people" I saw weren't just now-you-see-them-now-you-don't images. It was like they lived with me. They went about their daily lives as if they were normal and we weren't—but some of them had the nerve to talk back to me.

The reactions on other people's faces when I responded to these visions made me think I was crazy. I was embarrassed by my belief in these voices, and still am. I used to beg them to go away. Can you imagine this little Black girl with red hair talking to something no one else could see? I remember watching Casper the friendly ghost and thinking that he didn't look like the spirits I saw. I still wouldn't have played with Casper, though; he looked like a baby Klansman.

Anyway, as I grew older, I learned not to do anything that

would give me away. Now, as a grown-up with a Ph.D., I've accepted these experiences as real. I know that matter is neither created nor destroyed, though it does change form. The a cappella group Sweet Honey in the Rock sings a song that reminds us that the dead have never left us. They are not simply buried and forgotten under the earth. Instead, they are a part of the rustling of trees, the wailing of a child, a rock. We should learn to listen for them.

The spirits come to me less often now, and if they come at all, it's usually in my dreams. Sometimes what they tell me is confusing and frightening. I have spoken to God and said, Hello, God, sometimes this is more than I can bear. I don't know what to do with what I'm hearing. Please don't send these things to me. For now at least, She has granted my prayer. But if you see me somewhere talking to something you can't see, don't worry. I'm just talking to my ancestor—or yours. Do do do do do do do do (*Twilight Zone* music).

Finding a New Family

The people at the Mother Church of God in Christ took me in and loved me. Pop Pop and Nan Nan gave me love and shelter when I thought I didn't have any. I spent hours at their house every week, helping Nan Nan clean and move furniture when Pop Pop wasn't around to do it.

People often mistook Pop Pop's meekness for weakness. He was a quiet man, but brilliant, and without a weak bone in his body. He encouraged his parishioners to study and read beyond the teachings of the Bible, to read whatever books they could get their hands on—quite radical for a man of the Pentecostal cloth.

In our very demonstrative church, Pop Pop stood out in contrast. He didn't have the popular singsongy or hollering style of many Pentecostal preachers. At times you even had to lean forward to hear him, but his words were powerful. He taught us the importance of always giving thanks and praise to God. Instead of talking about what the devil wanted to do to us, he said we should speak of what God had done for us and helped us do for ourselves, of the good to come.

Pop Pop was my inspiration for the prayer I said before each *Bertice Berry Show*. I would gather our guests and staff together and say:

> *We affirm today that even in this crazy world of television*
> *We can have a positive impact,*
> *Touching the lives of not only those here*
> *But also of the people who will watch.*
> *We believe that some good will come of this*
> *And as always we believe that there is a possibility*
> *For growth, evolution, and change.*

People who'd been connected to other shows all told me that starting a TV show with a prayer was a new experience, but I felt it was the only way to keep myself and others focused on what we were there to do. I prayed with every person who appeared on that show, with the exception of a group of Satanists—I drew the line there.

Pop Pop died two years ago, but I know that he is still with me.

From Nan Nan I learned many other lessons. She is a dainty, quick-witted woman who could tell you off and keep smiling the whole time. She has a tremendous sense of style, and though the one I've developed for myself isn't an exact duplicate of hers, I do try to copy her sense of caring and detail, along with her belief in the value of good thoughts.

"Bertice," she'd say, "someday you will go to college and you have to take God there with you." I knew the part about taking God with me—or so I thought—but up to that point no one else had encouraged me to go to college. College was still an unspoken dream of mine, and here was Nan Nan helping me to speak it into existence.

A Closer Walk

I loved my church so much that between the ages of twelve and seventeen I spent nearly all my time there. My family often joked that I only came home to bathe. They accused me of being holier-than-thou. Many of my school friends also took up that refrain. I believe that friends are a gift from God. They are sent to help ease the burdens of everyday life and bring us peace.

During my junior high years I ended up finding friendship with two very different people. But they, too, were religiously dedicated, one to his synagogue and the other to books.

If I was overweight, Robert Katz was fat. He was also brilliant. Robert was one of the few White kids in my junior high school, and when I met him, I had only been inside a White person's home to clean it.

At first I thought Robert was a pest. I was the one who was supposed to be the first person with an answer to every question in class, but Robert kept beating me to it. Instead of becoming rivals, though, we became friends. First of all, it just so happened that we both got to school early in the morning. I came to school directly from cleaning jobs, Robert from Hebrew school.

On most days I'd meet him near his synagogue and we'd walk the rest of the way to school together as I pumped him for information about Judaism. Up until then I thought the word *jew* was a verb, something you did to store owners when you wanted to get a better deal. You *jewed* them down. When I realized that Jews were a group of people, I was embarrassed.

Robert opened my eyes to Jews as a community of people and to anti-Semitism. I began to take notice of all the despicable things that people said about Jews, and for me the most puzzling thing about this was why White people would say such things about other White people.

Robert loved Hebrew school. He was excited about the opportunity to learn about the Jewish faith and culture, and so was I. Through our talks, I began to recognize that though his faith was not exactly the same as mine, Jews, like Black people, were part of a culture that had kept its faith even through the experience of slavery and diaspora. Learning about Judaism and seeing the parallels with the history of my own people, I became determined that my faith would be an anchor for me, just as Robert's was for him and for his people.

Robert's friendship was an inspiration to me, while my relationship with another classmate, Chrystal, seemed like a constant test.

When I started writing this book, I soon realized that it was hard for me to remember my years in middle school, and that this was because of Chrystal. Like Robert, Chrystal was very bright and also somewhat quiet. She had the kind of Afro that my hair would never go into and a huge smile. Thinking about Chrystal makes me realize that most of my close friends are introverts around other people but are the extreme opposite around me. I don't know if I bring them out or if they shut me up. All I know is, we seem to switch roles when we're alone. I become quiet and they become talkative. Chrystal was truly like that. She had an opinion on everything—from her feelings about church to her intense critiques of everything she read or wrote.

Chrystal was my book pal. We read and discussed books, and we wrote poems about life, love, and God, and in Chrystal's case, about sadness and freedom.

One of our favorite writers was Edgar Allan Poe. I particularly loved "The Tell-Tale Heart," while Chrystal's favorite was "The Raven." Chrystal may have taken this to an extreme: Whenever someone asked her a question, she would answer, "Nevermore." It didn't matter what the question was.

Chrystal was an only child who was being raised by her father. She didn't talk about her mother, and I never asked for fear I would have to return the courtesy of an answer by talking about mine. I said earlier that we weren't allowed to talk about family matters outside of the house, but Chrystal was the kind of friend to whom you told everything. I knew if I ever got started with the slightest detail, I'd end up telling her all about my mother's alcoholism and abuse. I often witnessed to Chrystal, telling her how God could change her life, but when I invited her to church, she never came. I wasn't pushy about it, but in retrospect, perhaps I should have been.

One day after Chrystal and I had been friends for some time, my cousin Robin and I were walking to school and she asked me if I'd heard the news.

"What news?" I asked.

"Your friend Chrystal is dead," she said, rather casually.

The way she said it made me think Robin was playing one of her cruel practical jokes on me, so I didn't believe her. But when I got to school, the principal met me at the front door.

"In my office, Berry," he said.

I'd never been to the principal's office before. I tried to

think of what I'd done wrong, but I couldn't think of anything. Then I remembered what Robin had said and I realized she must have been telling the truth.

The police joined the principal and confirmed my fear: Chrystal was dead; she had shot herself the night before.

The police wanted to know if I knew anything about it. What could I have known? I was just twelve years old and my best friend had blown her brains out. There had been no telltale signs, no drug use or obvious depression. I'd seen no change in her attitude, anger or the opposite. There was nothing. All I knew was that my friend Chrystal was smart and beautiful and that I'd never see her alive again. I wondered whom I'd tell my secrets to now and whom I'd read books and write poems with. *Nevermore.*

They read me a note she'd left, but to me it sounded like one of her poems about loneliness.

Another one of her friends told me that Chrystal had tried to kill herself before. "She never told me that," I said, crying. The other girl said that Chrystal wouldn't have told me because she knew how much I loved God and life.

We were sent to class and that was it. No one discussed Chrystal any further or tried to give us any special counseling. I began to have nightmares about Chrystal in which she was calling me and asking me to save her. I felt guilty about her suicide and wished that I had talked to her even more than I had, that I'd asked her about her mother, made her come to church. I wished that she could be still alive so that we could grow up together and tell stories to the children we would have.

But as my mother says, "If wishes were dreams, horses *could* fly."

There wasn't much of a positive nature to be learned from Chrystal's death, but her short life had taught me to cherish my own. To live it to the fullest and to treat every encounter with everyone as if it were the last. This was a tough lesson for a twelve-year-old, but a valuable one. My friends say that they can always rely on me to make them feel better.

God Works in Mysterious Ways

Nan Nan and Pop Pop didn't know the whole story, but they knew my situation at home wasn't good; and often they prayed with me as I implored God to take away my mother's drinking. My mother's friendship with the bottle was a great test of my faith.

I tried to get Mom to attend church with me, but she accused me of turning against her and said that church people were always judging others and thought they were better than everybody else. Some of what she said was true. Sometimes the saints could gossip with the best of them.

Before I left Wilmington for college, I went to my mother and told her that I was never coming back to her house until she stopped drinking. I had decided that while I'd had no control over my childhood, I would over the rest of my life and I was going to be happy. I didn't want any further part of it. I told her that she shouldn't even bother to call me with the news that some-one in the family had died. It was harsh and maybe even cruel, but I was disgusted and felt like I was at the end of my rope.

I headed off to Jacksonville with my words to my mother echoing in my head. But I also remembered the advice Pop Pop had given me from the Scriptures: "God works in myste-rious ways."

Like anybody who encounters a wealth of new information and new ideas, in college I began to examine many of the principles that I'd trusted in and lived by. Inevitably, I began to question my religious beliefs. I began to wonder if God even existed, and if She did, why She'd allowed Black folks to be so oppressed. I also began to question why God hadn't answered my many prayers for my mother's recovery from alcoholism.

I thought about all of this, and of how far I'd come, and gradually my faith returned and began to grow stronger. I realized that though everything in my life wasn't perfect, it was God who had enabled me to get to college and have these thoughts in the first place.

I often got into debates about the existence of God with one of my professors, who was more skeptical.

"How do you know there is a God?" he or she would ask.

"Because I talk to Her," I would reply.

"If there is a God, what does She tell you?"

"That there's hope for you White folks yet."

"What's your proof that there's a God?"

"Because I feel God's presence."

"But you can't see it."

"And you can't see the wind."

We had more than one of these encounters.

Between my faith in myself and in God, I felt capable of meeting any challenge, no matter how daunting. I knew, in the abstract at least, that I would never face anything I was not somehow ready to deal with.

So when I received my first letter from my mother, I thought my heart would burst. The letter was short, and a bit awkward, as if she wasn't sure how I would react to it. But the point was that it was a letter, a gesture from my mother, who was clearly reaching out to me.

And I reached right back. God had opened up a door that I had tried to slam shut. So if I had any thoughts about taking a hard line with my mother, I thought that since God had opened the door, who was I to try to close it again?

The letters started to come regularly. In one letter she said that she'd missed me and wished I would visit. I called her and we talked for quite a while, and among other things, she told me that she had stopped drinking and had begun going to church. It was an important moment.

I'd waited all my life to hear the news she was delivering, but now that she was saying it, I somehow didn't know how to respond. I was even kind of suspicious and wondered if she was just telling me this to make me feel better. She thanked me for pushing her, and I asked her how she'd done it. Was she attending AA meetings?

She said that she'd just awakened one morning and decided that her life had to change. She'd stopped drinking cold turkey—and Wild Turkey, too. For support she'd gone back to church.

After I got over my initial skepticism, I felt overjoyed. The prayers I'd prayed as a young girl were being answered. Gradually I saw that as my mother got her life together, my family began to grow closer again.

Once again, God had heard me. But I knew that God wasn't going to rearrange the world for me, and that if I wanted changes, it was up to me to make them happen.

If Two or Three Are Gathered . . .

God did see to it that I continued to be blessed with friends who shared my faith and helped me with my journey, even though I sometimes had to work hard to find them. One such friend was Rhonda Williams, whom I got to know in college and whose friendship was one of the more unlikely I have ever formed.

It was unlikely because people would see us together and shake their heads. I was seen as being a somewhat wild intellectual, spouting sociological theory, dancing with abandon when I was joyful, and shouting with equal abandon when I was angry. Rhonda has always had a peaceful dignity and a reserved bearing that come from her ever-graceful spirit, which makes people assume she is the product of an elegant upper-class upbringing.

In reality, Rhoda grew up in the Farragut Houses, in one of Brooklyn's toughest neighborhoods, but she got both her faith and her poise from her parents, who happen to be two of the most generous souls on the planet.

Together, Rhonda and I formed a singing duet that performed at many of Jacksonville's churches and special events. We also shared an apartment, attended graduate school together, and kept our faith alive through the ministry of our singing.

I found other good friends, too, often through weird circumstances. Once, a young man I'd met in the library dropped by my apartment to "chat." Once inside, he was all over me, and as hard as I fought, he still thought I was playing hard to get. For some reason I was afraid to scream, and, I'm ashamed to say, I was actually worried about what my neighbors would think, since I'd let him in.

Meantime, I pleaded with him to stop and to leave me alone, and finally I did convince him by saying it wasn't a good time of the month. He left, but before he did, he extracted a promise from me to go out with him the following week. Then I quickly locked the door behind him.

I cried and cried, feeling guilty and dirty at the same time. I wondered what I'd done to lead him on and worried that maybe I'd sent him the wrong signals. About an hour after he'd left, my friend Molly Carver called, and I realized I needed to talk to someone. I was glad to hear her voice.

Molly was a young White woman from a large family in San-dusky, Ohio. Her father had been an educator and her mom a homemaker. She never tried to "act Black" just because we were friends. She never asked stupid race questions. She wasn't like other Whites I'd known who thought that because they knew someone Black, they also knew everything there was to know about Black history. She educated herself: "Since it's a Black thing and I don't understand, I am going to find out," she'd say.

That night after the attempted attack, I asked Molly to come over and she did. I told her what had happened and she helped me to recognize that I wasn't at fault. Even though I knew this in my head, Molly helped me realize it in my heart.

After this episode, it took me a long time to get back to my normal routine. The only time I went out was to dash to class and then rush back home. I was afraid to go to the police. I hadn't been physically raped, so I was afraid that if I went to the police, nothing would be done.

Several months later I was feeling better and had left the shelter of my apartment, and I ran right into the guy who had accosted me. He immediately started talking in loud tones about the date we were supposed to go on. He went on to accuse me of preferring White men and ended by telling me I wasn't a real sister.

By this time I was stronger, and I was determined to no longer keep this to myself. I told a group of my women friends about what had happened, and they took action. They took turns calling this guy around the clock and warning him that he'd better not try anything with me again. We distributed material that subtly pointed out that if he ever pulled something like that again, we'd kick his ass and we'd be wearing high-heeled shoes while doing it.

I confided in several male friends who really stood by me during this time. For example, Anthony Floyd and Paul Green had noticed that I'd stopped coming regularly to the gym, and they wanted to know why. They asked Molly, and she told them what had happened. Then they came to me to find out how far they could go: They wanted to punish him, and they were serious. I told them that I didn't want them to use violence on my behalf, particularly since Anthony was like a fifty-eleventh-degree black belt. They reluctantly agreed to give up their plan for vengeance, but they continued to check on me periodically and would harass my attacker. Sometimes they'd follow the guy and whisper sweet nothings in his ear when they got close enough.

After our little campaign, several other women came forward; some weren't as lucky as I was. Anthony and Paul convinced this guy to change his ways. I don't know how, and I don't want to either.

I've learned that having good friends, people who are positive and resourceful, is necessary in order to stay on your own path. Without them, you don't always have the strength to go forward. With them you can truly see your way clear.

At Kent State I began to attend a local church, hoping for the kind of support I'd received in Jacksonville and at my Wilmington church. This new church had a small, predominately White congregation, many of whom were also part of the campus community. There were many good Christian folks, but eventually their involvement or call shifted from a focus on strengthening their families and communities to single-minded participation in protests against abortion. I kept wondering exactly how and when this shift had taken place. They seemed to see it as a necessary part of their Christianity, but I didn't agree.

Pop Pop had taught me that we were living in a time of the Dispensation of Grace. What he meant was that this was a period in history different from others in that each individual has an opportunity to choose God's love. But while I could understand the need to witness and bring others to Christ— that was, after all, our duty as Christians—what I didn't understand was trying to force our morality on others. Nor could I understand why the congregation hadn't spent as much time on issues such as racial discrimination or poverty as they had on issues like abortion.

I discussed my concerns with one of the pastors and also with a few of the members. They correctly pointed out that their work was probably not what I was meant to do, that I hadn't been called to that purpose, but that I shouldn't doubt God and my faith because of this. I told them it wasn't God I was doubting, but as much as I'd come to like this church and its wonderful praise service, I already knew I had to leave.

But again, good things sprang from a bad situation—it was when I felt forced to change churches that I found new friends in my new congregation, and it was they who cheered me on at my dissertation defense. I might not have gotten through that defense if I had remained in the first church and spent my time struggling internally with my misgivings about their mission. I knew this was God's way of showing me that the paths through life are manifold and that it's our duty to find the right one.

Finding the Proper Joy

When I got my Ph.D., I gave thanks to God and knew that I should celebrate. (By the way, isn't it strange that after his acquittal for the murders of Ron Goldman and Nicole Brown Simpson, O. J. Simpson didn't go running into the nearest church to thank God—any God?) Anyway, I wanted to do something that would commemorate my achievement and reward me for my hard work.

Initially I had promised myself the reward of one-carat diamond earrings. I'd read that certain tribes in Africa would pierce their ears only after they had done something of major significance. I knew that in the eighteenth century sailors pierced an ear only after they had sailed around the world or survived a significant shipwreck. My achievement was pretty clear. Getting a Ph.D. was like surviving a shipwreck.

I had pierced my right ear when I'd passed my comprehensive exams, another tough journey. Now I was eager to pierce my left ear so that people would stop asking me stupid questions like, "What does it mean to have only one earring? Are you gay or something?"

But then I recalled reading about the horrible conditions in the diamond mines in South Africa—the work was full of danger for its barely paid work. And I knew that most of the diamonds imported by the United States came from South Africa, which still operated under apartheid. Was this something I wanted to be reminded of every time I thought about my Ph.D.?

In thinking about my reward to myself, I was also challenged by something Alice Walker had written. She said, "If we value that which is plentiful over that which is scarce, then the revolution can take place." I decided that I didn't need diamond earrings after all, that I would rather put shells in my ears than diamonds. And that's what I did. Now whenever I put those earrings on, they mean something; they are symbols of all that I value, love, and respect. They remind me of the qualities that I know God wants me to feel in myself. And they remind me that the revolution is coming.

Once when I was on the comedy road, driving through the Florida panhandle, for one reason or another I was doubting myself and my work. During this doubt session, I was listening to Bob Marley's "Try Jah Love."

I began to pray and to ask God what my true purpose was. In the past, I had frequently asked God what to do in any given circumstance, but I hadn't given extensive thought to my overall purpose in life. Dr. Na'im Akbar, a Black psychologist, talks about the need to ask yourself, Why am I here now? I began to meditate on this question. I got my answer. God instructed me to be happy.

I thought this was the devil speaking, so I prayed again.

God said, "Yo, it's me. I want you to be happy and to share that happiness with others."

Always one for a good debate, I then asked, So, what is sin?

In reply God said, "That which makes you unhappy."

This idea was startling in its simplicity, but I deeply felt its truth. It's amazing how some of the most complicated things are really quite simple—like math.

I started thinking about the best relationships between parents and their children, the kind where parents want to see their child happy and will do almost anything to make it so. But these parents also know that for their child to be happy, there are things the child must avoid, so the parents protect the child for as long as possible. Eventually the child must begin to experience things for himself. So the parent says, "Don't do this, don't do that," and the child asks, "Why?" And the parents say, "Because it's not good for you. It will make you unhappy."

Once when I shared this view with a friend, he accused me of being a hedonist. I pointed out that I worked far too hard to say that pleasure was my only goal, but that I also did not want to be trapped in a world of dos and don'ts.

I've always wanted to try and live and operate within God's perfect plan for my life, but it was only as I got older that I realized God's will is not as rigid as I had thought. There are countless ways to work within this plan, countless choices that will enable me to service Her will and my happiness at the same time.

I've discovered that what makes me happy is entertaining and educating at the same time. The way I go about this has already changed several times, and I'll probably find many other variations before I'm done. But because I feel God's blessing every time I work to fulfill my purpose, and because I believe that everything in my life up to this point has prepared me for it, I have no doubt that I have found the path God hoped I would follow.

Peace.

Afterword

*L*ife is a series of paths. The meaning of the life is in the process of the path. By simply living, we begin to learn our purpose. But we must examine our living every step of the way.

The simple process of writing this book (which, now that I think of it, was anything but simple) has enabled me to understand many things that once were major life mysteries for me. I now realize the connection between my life and the unfulfilled longings of my ancestors. The sins of the parents are passed on to the children. I've come to understand that the more we can know about them, the more we can know about ourselves, and only then can we begin to complete the necessary cycles and end the unnecessary, detrimental ones.

Now that I've begun to ask questions, my family continues to come forward with all kinds of wonderful facts. "Child, did you know that Aunt Goldie made her own false teeth?" "Out of wood?" I asked. "No, fool, everybody knows that you make false teeth out of wax." "Oh, yeah."

I recently learned from my sister Chris that my grandmother once shot at a man with a double-barreled shotgun. The man was a neighbor who had been beating his wife, and my grandmother just got sick of it. When the police came to question her about the shooting, she told them that she didn't know what they were talking about. Her neighbors protected her by hiding the shotgun, and since there was no damage beyond a broken window, the police decided to leave her alone. My grandmother said they were wrong, that the real damage was to a woman who had been battered.

The three children are also teaching me, especially about the delicate balance between love and discipline. When my friends ask if I give the kids an allowance, I tell them, "Yes. I allow them to live here."

I've learned many things, some sought after, some accidental. I hope that passing on the lessons of my process can help you through yours. After all, we are all connected. I am because you are. When I first got my talk show, reporters compared me to Oprah and then had the nerve to ask if I took that as an insult. I told them no and that if it hadn't been for Oprah and all her success, no one would have considered me for television in the first place.

I've accomplished much, but I know that I'm standing on the shoulders of giants. I'm not the only one, nor am I the first, but I've been prepared and the time is right.

The process of writing has also enabled me to recognize the need to take matters into my own hands. My purpose in life is not up to television executives or booking agents. It is up to me. I've been given many gifts and talents. We all have. If we don't use them, we lose them.

Here is a list of things that have helped me to enjoy the process of life, things I try to do every day. I pass them on to you.

- Pray
- Tell myself that I love me

- Get thirteen to three hundred hugs a day—they help to keep me from becoming a sociopath
- Compliment somebody
- Read
- Exercise (you don't need a gym, a treadmill or a trainer—walk!)
- Write down something that happened or something I want to happen
- Try to eat right and drink plenty of water
- Smell good—people will like you
- Smile at people you don't know
- Tell the folks who've made an impact, "Thank you"
- Be informed
- Talk to myself
- Listen to music and make some of my own
- Work for peace

I hope that my life lessons can help you with yours.

Oh, yeah, you know the riddle on page 58—the one about the man in the room. It was suicide, and he stood on a block of ice. Sorry to keep you hanging (no pun intended).

Peace!